For such a
time as this

For such a time as this

time as this

A renewed diaconate in the Church of England

A report to the General Synod of the Church of England
of a Working Party of the House of Bishops

GS 1407

CHURCH HOUSE
PUBLISHING

Church House Publishing
Church House
Great Smith Street
London
SW1P 3NZ

Published 2001 for the House of
Bishops by Church House
Publishing

GS 1407

Typeset in 10pt Sabon
Cover design by Visible Edge
Printed by Creative Print and
Design Group, Ebbw Vale, Wales

*This report has only the authority
of the Group that produced it.*

ISBN: 978-0-7151-4347-6

Contents

Membership of the Renewed Diaconate Working Party

The Rt Revd Barry Rogerson
Bishop of Bristol   (Chairman)

Deacon Margaret Crompton   Members
The Methodist Church

The Revd Canon Professor Robert Hannaford

The Revd Dr Paul McPartlan
The Roman Catholic Church

Mr Richard Noble

The Revd Roy Overthrow

The Very Revd Stephen Platten

The Revd Deacon Ann Wren

The Revd Prebendary Dr Paul Avis   Staff
General Secretary, Council for Christian Unity

The Venerable Dr Gordon Kuhrt
Director, Ministry Division

Dr Martin Davie
Theological Secretary of CCU,
Theological Consultant to the House of Bishops

Foreword by the Chairman

Across the Christian traditions and around the world the churches are rediscovering the diaconate. From Cologne to Cape Town and from Vancouver to Vienna, among Roman Catholics, Lutherans, Methodists and Anglicans, deacons are to be found playing a vital role in enabling the people of God to exercise their personal and corporate discipleship. The exercise of sacrificial love is a vital part of the mission of the Church and deacons are both a sign and an agent of such love.

The Deanery of Huntingdon in the Diocese of Ely caught this vision and the Ely Diocesan Synod brought it to the General Synod in November 1998. The Synod requested the House of Bishops to set up a Working Party on a renewed diaconate and to take into account recent developments in lay and ordained ministry.

This report is the result of three years' work involving not only Anglicans but representatives of the Roman Catholic and Methodist Churches. The Working Party has built on the work done by previous working parties on the diaconate, particularly the report of 1988. But it has also drawn on contemporary biblical, doctrinal and liturgical studies as well as on the practical experience of many churches. The emerging findings of the Working Party have been shared with Anglican and ecumenical partners and found to be in harmony with much of what is developing elsewhere.

The Working Party has gladly taken to heart the concern of the General Synod that the renewed diaconate should be seen in the context of developing lay ministries, especially those of Reader and Lay Pastoral Assistant. These valued ministries are affirmed, not undermined, in the report. It is clear that the phenomenon of 'overlap' is to be found in all the authorized ministries of the Church of England. It is not an issue that is specific to the diaconate. What is being proposed here is an order of ministry that is versatile in support of the mission of the Church.

The theological theme that has held this work together is that of Jesus the Deacon of God, whose ministers represent Jesus the Deacon to the world, but also enable the people of God in their diaconal responsibility of worship, prayer and care. Such deacons help to link the worshipping heart of the Church to a needy world.

The report stands in continuity with the Anglican tradition and in particular with the Church of England's Ordinals. We envisage a distinctive diaconate alongside the so-called 'transitional' diaconate. But we believe that our report has implications for all deacons. All clergy are ordained to the diaconate, but some of us in the Church of England have only a vague idea of what that means. There are already many distinctive deacons in our Church. What we offer is a theological grounding that takes account of recent biblical studies, a vision of the renewed diaconate at the cutting edge of the Church's mission, combined with realistic guidelines for good practice. Above all, our hope is that this report will encourage and enable the mission of the whole people of God.

Finally, our thanks go to the secretariat of the Working Party: Prebendary Paul Avis and Dr Martin Davie.

✠ Barry Bristol
Chairman

chapter 1

Introduction

This report makes comprehensive proposals for the renewal of the diaconate in the Church of England. Its authors believe that the diaconate needs to be taken altogether more seriously in the Church of England instead of being taken for granted much of the time, and should not be seen as merely a transitional stage on the way to the priesthood or presbyterate. They are convinced that the diaconate can be rediscovered as a distinctive, permanent ministry for some ordained ministers and as the fundamental commissioning of all ordained ministers.

The title of this report *For such a time as this* is, of course, taken from Esther 4.14 (AV). The Greek translation (Septuagint, LXX) of the Hebrew Bible used the word *kairos*: it stands for a significant, pregnant moment, a decisive moment in God's time. It seems that the diaconate has been particularly important in the Church's mission at times of acute political and social change and upheaval.

In fourth and fifth century Rome, deacons rose to the challenge of providing social welfare after the capital of the Western empire was moved from Rome to Ravenna to escape the advancing Germanic tribes. During the upheavals of the Reformation period, *diakonia* connected the feeding of the Eucharist to the need to feed the armies of displaced beggars. In the early nineteenth century, the aftermath of the Napoleonic wars, rapid industrialization and vast movements of population from the country to the cities left many in poverty. In these circumstances the ministry of the deacon or deaconess emerged with greater clarity. At the beginning of the twenty-first century, the failure of welfare services in parts of Northern Europe and North America, changes to the political geography of Eastern Europe and the sense of the widening gap between the Church and the communities to whom it seeks to minister in an increasingly secular and plural society, have fostered a renewal of the diaconate in the service of the Church's mission.

Although the Working Party senses strongly that there is a new urgency about the ministry of deacons in the mission of the Church, it develops its argument in continuity with the Church of England's ordinals of 1550/1662 and 1980. But it draws on ecumenical insights, from Vatican II to the Anglican–Lutheran Hanover Report, and on recent discoveries in biblical scholarship, to sharpen the focus of diaconal ministry. Particularly significant perhaps is the attention paid by the report to the demands of mission in an increasingly post-Christian culture and to the range of opportunities in evangelism, pastoral outreach and social involvement that would be appropriate for deacons as envisaged here.

After laying ecumenical, theological and biblical foundations and drawing attention to the mission context of ministry today, the report explores the issue of how a renewed diaconate would relate to recent developments in lay and ordained ministry. It affirms the ministry of Readers and Lay Parish Assistants and relates its thinking to Local Ministry Teams and to the emergence of Ordained Local Ministry. What it offers is a view of diaconal ministry that is distinctive but not exclusive. It acknowledges that the issue of 'overlap' is pervasive in the delineation of ministries. The report goes on to offer a basic ministerial profile, a sort of job description, of distinctive deacons. It sets out both what, in the view of the Working Party, they should and should not do. Finally, the report addresses some practical consequences of its recommendations – issues of selection, training and deployment – setting out some guidelines for the appropriate committees of the Ministry Division, under the oversight of the House of Bishops, to develop.

This is the report of a Working Party of the House of Bishops of the Church of England, which has collegial responsibility for the ministry of the word, the sacraments and pastoral care. The Working Party was set up by the General Synod in November 1998, through an initiative of the Ely Diocesan Synod. It reports to the Synod through the House of Bishops and the Archbishops' Council. The group has met eight times, three of them residentially, during 1999–2001. A feature of the Working

Party is the presence of ecumenical members from the Roman Catholic and Methodist Churches. The group shared its emerging findings with Anglican and ecumenical representatives from a range of churches and diaconal organizations at a Consultation at St George's House, Windsor Castle, under the auspices of the Centre for the Study of the Christian Church in April 2001, and was confirmed in the direction it was taking. The Ministry Division and the Council for Christian Unity have been involved through their Director and General Secretary respectively.

The proposals that follow have significant implications for the mission and ministry of the Church of England in the twenty-first century. They are offered 'for such a time as this' (cf. Esther 4.14 [AV]).

chapter 2

The diaconate in history and today

How the current form of the diaconate came about

The apostolic and post-apostolic period

A threefold pattern of ministry can be discerned in the apostolic age
(cf. Preface to the 1662 Ordinal; Canon C 1. 1). Within the New
Testament itself, we find Apostles and apostolic delegates such as
Timothy and Titus exercising what is recognizably an episcopal ministry,
together with presbyters or overseers, and also deacons (along with
other ministries such as that of evangelist, prophet and teacher).
Beginning in early post-apostolic times, however, a threefold ordained
ministry gradually became accepted as the universal norm in the Church.
As the most broadly based and widely received ecumenical agreement
recognizes: 'During the second and third centuries a threefold pattern of
bishop, presbyter and deacon became established as the pattern of
ordained ministry throughout the Church' (*Baptism, Eucharist and
Ministry* [*BEM*], 1982, M19). In fact many Christian traditions
throughout the history of the Church reflect this model: the model of a
senior pastor of the community, collegial associates of the pastor and
pastoral assistants to carry out ministry in the world (as the House of
Bishops' statement *Eucharistic Presidency,*1997 has noted: 3.16). This
pattern has been identified as 'personal, collegial and communal' and as
such has entered into the ecumenical bloodstream (*BEM*, M26).

Historical variety and a common thread

The ministry of deacons has taken many varied forms in the history of
the Christian Church. There is no single normative model of the

diaconate to which we can hark back. Which particular snapshot of the diaconate in history would we choose? As Bishop Stephen Sykes said in the General Synod debate that commissioned this report: 'Any attempt to restore a supposed traditional diaconate would involve a more or less arbitrary decision about which of the diverse forms was to be taken as normative' (General Synod, *Report of Proceedings*, November 1998, p. 856). However, although models of diaconal ministry have been quite diverse it is possible to discern a unifying principle.

A striking feature of the diaconate, viewed historically, has been its flexibility, its capacity to be adapted to the changing needs of the Church and society. It has been the least specific, the most malleable, of the three orders. In rethinking diaconal ministry it is important not to lose that flexibility but rather to be somewhat relaxed about the different directions that the diaconate has taken and could take again. The prudent householder brings out of his or her treasures things new and old (Matthew 13.52). The responsiveness to changing needs, that has been the hallmark of the diaconal order, may be the key to its relevance today. The need at the present time may well be to find an overarching rationale that brings together the diverse roles – liturgical, pastoral, communal, administrative, catechetical and prophetic – that *diakonia* (diaconal ministry) has taken in the Church's life. Though models of diaconal ministry have been varied, the guiding thread seems to be the *connecting* nature of the diaconate. It has tended to be an order of ministry poised between the sacred liturgy of the Church, presided over by the bishop and the bishop's presbyters, and the down-to-earth needs of a world longing (whether it knows it or not) for the salvation of God. In our report, this becomes the key principle, which is then worked out in various concrete ways.

The diaconate in the English Church

It is not necessary to rehearse once again the chequered history of the diaconate in the English Church (this section draws substantially on *Deacons in the Ministry of the Church*, 1988, pp. 11ff; cf. also Brodd, 1999). Medieval deacons were in major, not minor orders and came to be bound to celibacy. Deacons had a mainly liturgical function, assisting the priest at the Eucharist, and (with permission) preaching and baptizing. Alongside their liturgical role, deacons acquired administrative responsibilities on behalf of the bishop. Generally, the diaconate became extremely attenuated, a transitional period of a few weeks *en route* to the priesthood. However, there were permanent deacons, often in academic posts, and archdeacons were really deacons (as they still are in the Orthodox tradition), administering discipline on behalf of the bishop. When, as often happened, the archdeacon was elected to the see on the death of the bishop, he would be ordained priest before being consecrated bishop.

At the Reformation, the English Church continued uninterrupted the historic threefold ordained ministry and the diaconate remained transitional to the priesthood. Deacons were Clerks in Holy Orders and, at a time when the Eucharist was celebrated only three or four times a year in parish churches and private confession was widely disused, deacons could perform most clerical functions. Until the Act of Uniformity of 1662, deacons were frequently instituted to benefices. After 1662 bishops tended to ordain men to the diaconate and the presbyterate on the same day, or within a few days, in order to license them to the sole charge of a parish, either as incumbents or as curates serving on behalf of an absent incumbent.

The historic Ordinal

The Ordinal of 1550, as revised in 1662 and bound with *The Book of Common Prayer*, remains a doctrinal standard for the Church of England. It defines the ministry of deacons thus:

> It appertaineth to the office of a Deacon, in the church where he shall be appointed to serve, to assist the Priest in Divine Service, and specially when he ministereth the Holy Communion, and to help him in the distribution thereof; and to read Holy Scriptures and Homilies in the church; and to instruct the youth in the Catechism; in the absence of the Priest to baptize infants; and to preach, if he be admitted thereto by the Bishop. And furthermore, it is his office, where provision is so made, to search for the sick, poor, and impotent people of the Parish, to intimate their estates, names, and places where they dwell, unto the Curate, that by his exhortation they may be relieved with the alms of the Parishioners, or others.

We take this statement as a benchmark for our work on the renewed diaconate. The Ordinal here describes an estimable ministry for the deacon. It is essentially a ministry involving word and sacrament and compassionate pastoral care. Though the aspect of authoritative commissioning is muted in the Ordinal, diaconal ministry is clearly exercised on behalf of the bishop, the incumbent ('Curate') and the parish. The text of the Ordinal suggests a movement of reaching out from the liturgical heart of parish life to those who are estranged by poverty or sickness, rallying the resources of the parish to meet their need. (The converse of this, the reciprocal movement from the needs and concerns of the world to the eucharistic heart of the Church, through the ministry of the deacon, is a later insight and is not adequately brought out in the Ordinal.) There is no necessary implication that the diaconate is transitional. In the Ordinal, the ministry of the deacon has value and integrity in itself. This present report builds on the Ordinal's understanding of diaconal ministry and takes it as the foundation of its work.

The current Ordinal

In the nineteenth century, with the emergence of a new sense of professionalism among the clergy and growing awareness of huge pastoral needs in large urban parishes, the diaconate as then understood was taken more seriously. One consequence was, however, that the diaconate came to be seen as a probationary year during which the apprentice priest learned his professional duties. Thus, in one sense, the diaconate was strengthened by being given a more professional definition. But in another sense it was weakened, as these developments had the effect of reinforcing the 'transitional' model of the diaconate. However, the development of the deaconess orders pointed to the possibilities of a distinctive diaconal ministry.

The revision of the Ordinal in *The Alternative Service Book 1980* gave a slightly different slant to the office and work of a deacon than *The Book of Common Prayer*. The emphasis is on service, liturgical functions and working with the church's members in caring for those in need. Not only the poor but also the backsliders among the parishioners are the deacon's concern. There is perhaps a more corporate sense of the deacon acting on behalf of the whole body. (The use of the masculine pronoun dates this ordinal before the admission of women to the ordained diaconate.)

A deacon is called to serve the Church of God, and to work with its members in caring for the poor, the needy, the sick and all who are in trouble. He is to strengthen the faithful, search out the careless and indifferent, and to preach the word of God in the place to which he is licensed. A deacon assists the priest under whom he serves, in leading the worship of the people, especially in the administration of the Holy Communion. He may baptize when required to do so. It is his general duty to do such pastoral work as is entrusted to him.

Recent history

In 1974 the Advisory Committee for the Church's Ministry (ACCM) produced a report that was unable to find a convincing theological rationale for the diaconate and recommended abolishing it altogether. The 1977 debate in General Synod declined to follow this advice, but 'took note of' a further report which set out a range of options. In 1986 the House of Bishops of the General Synod commissioned further work under the chairmanship of the then Bishop of Portsmouth, co-authored by Dr Mary Tanner and the present Dean of Norwich: *Deacons in the Ministry of the Church* (1988).

By 1987 some 700 women (most previously serving as deaconesses or lay workers) had been ordained as deacons, with no immediate prospect of becoming priests, and there was an urgent need to understand this development theologically. The report provided substantial historical and theological resources for study of the diaconate and recommended the setting up of a distinctive or permanent diaconate, with a ministry of word and sacrament. The accent was strongly on a ministry of self-giving service to others (see p. 78ff). Though this was not the report's intention, it was assumed by many that most candidates for ordination to a permanent diaconate would be women.

The legislation providing for the ordination of women to the priesthood/presbyterate in 1992, with the first ordinations in 1994, immediately dated some of the assumptions behind the commissioning of this report. Its proposals have been carried forward in only one or two dioceses. (A distinctive diaconate is still relevant to that constituency in the Church of England that is looking for a permanent 'non-headship' ministry for women: see p. 47f.) Although the Church of England as a whole has not come to terms fully with the advent of women priests, it is now perhaps possible to reconsider the central proposal of *Deacons in the Ministry of the Church* on its theological and pastoral merits in a way that is not overshadowed by the question of the ordination of women priests.

The present position in the Church of England

The changed situation with regard to women priests is not the only new factor since 1988. Developments in ecumenical theology, changes in society, an enhanced missiological awareness, developments in lay ministry and new theological insights, based on New Testament research, call for a fresh appraisal of the diaconate. However, a sensible approach will not attempt to duplicate earlier work, which retains its value, but to build on it.

The present position in the Church of England, defined by the Ordinals and Canons, is that the diaconate is (as will be explained below) in essence a *non-presidential representative ministry of word, sacrament and pastoral care*. It is theologically important that all clergy are ordained deacon. In the catholic understanding of holy order, presbyters and bishops do not leave their diaconal ordination behind them (just as bishops do not leave behind their ordination to the priesthood). The diaconate remains a fundamental stratum, so to speak, whatever more is added to one's ministry (see Wright, 'Sequential or Cumulative Orders vs. Direct Ordination',1993). This truth is often invoked to emphasize the servant nature of presbyteral and episcopal ministry, and this, of course, remains valid. But the diaconal foundation of all ordained ministry becomes all the more important when it is seen in the light of the recent rediscovery of the biblical idea of *diakonia* (see p. 31f).

However, in the Church of England, the diaconate remains predominantly a transitional stage to the priesthood, with the almost inevitable consequence that deacons are widely regarded as serving an 'apprenticeship' before being 'promoted to higher things'. When the diaconate is seen as simply transitional, it is difficult to avoid slipping into the assumption that there are hierarchical degrees of ministry, stepping stones from one to the next, rather than distinctive callings, within the total ministry of the people of God – callings that are equal in value within the divine economy.

What is already possible

Nevertheless, in the Church of England, ordination to a distinctive or permanent diaconate is already possible, within the scope of the Ordinal and Canons. It is thought (see Deacon C. Hall in *The Ministry of the Deacon*, 1999, pp. 201ff) that there are currently about 75 active distinctive deacons in the Church of England, of whom two-thirds are women. Many work in a secular environment, in communities or institutions. All deacons in the Church of England are licensed to preach, but their liturgical role is not always fully exercised. Nearly half of all active distinctive deacons are in the dioceses of Portsmouth, Chichester and London.

Vocations to a distinctive diaconate are carefully considered on their merits by national selectors in consultation with the sponsoring bishop. However, at present there are no separate national criteria for the selection of distinctive deacons and no separate national guidelines for their training or deployment. The Bishop Otter Centre for Theology and Ministry, within University College, Chichester, though not accredited by the House of Bishops for ordination training, is the only Anglican institution specializing in the training of distinctive deacons (though an ecumenical formation for deacons is provided by The Queen's College, Birmingham). It is probable, of course, that central provision and encouragement in these areas would foster an increase in vocations.

chapter 3

Ecumenical developments in theology and practice

For several years, the diaconal ministry of the Church, and specifically the ministry of Deacons, has been a major topic of theological research and discussion throughout the Christian churches. Across the ecumenical spectrum, the diaconate has been the subject of re-thinking, reform and renewal. The diaconate has been described as 'an escalating phenomenon' (Brodd in *The Ministry of the Deacon 1*, 1999, pp. 11ff). As a consequence of liturgical renewal, missiological awareness, developments in the theological understanding of representative ministry, and discoveries in New Testament research, the diaconate has been reinvigorated in many parts of the Church (*The Diaconate as Ecumenical Opportunity*: Hanover Report: 1).

The ecumenical picture

The Roman Catholic Church

Within the Roman Catholic Church since Vatican II, there has been provision for a distinctive diaconate for men (who may be married) as a ministry of word, sacrament and charity (*Lumen Gentium*, 29). Those who are called to the diaconate become the permanent and committed 'servants of the mysteries of Christ and the Church' (*ibid.*, 41). The ministry of deacons has developed permissively in proportion to the enthusiasm of diocesan bishops for this ministry.

In 1998, two major documents on the permanent diaconate were issued by the Congregation for Catholic Education and the Congregation for the Clergy in the Vatican 'to clarify and regulate the diversity of approaches adopted in experiments conducted up to now' ('Joint Declaration' introducing the *Basic Norms for the Formation of Permanent Deacons* and *Directory for the Ministry and Life of Permanent Deacons*, 1998). On the basis of these documents, the Roman Catholic Bishops' Conference of England and Wales, and other bishops' conferences around the world, are producing national directories on the permanent diaconate. The deacon is described as 'a living icon of Christ the servant within the Church' (*Basic Norms*, 11) and 'a driving force for service' (*ibid.*, 5). He has an integrated ministry of word, altar and charity: 'ministry of the word leads to ministry at the altar, which in turn prompts the transformation of life by the liturgy, resulting in charity' (*Directory*, 39). The deacon bridges the liturgical and caritative tasks of the Church. On the one hand, he helps the people 'to unite their lives to the offering of Christ', while on the other hand, 'in the name of Christ himself, he helps the Church to participate in the fruits of that sacrifice' (*ibid.*, 28), and 'to exercise its mission of charity' (*ibid.*, 40). Deacons often support and coordinate the work of lay people. Friedrichshafen, in Germany, is a striking example of Roman Catholic parishes working together to provide diaconal ministry, grounded in the Eucharist, to the needy of the city by means of deacons who lead teams of lay volunteers.

The Lutheran tradition

The strong Lutheran tradition of *diakonia* has referred primarily to the Church's social outreach, often from an institutional base. The ministry of deacons is sometimes exclusively pastoral (as we would tend to say), rather than a ministry concerned with teaching and assisting with the sacraments. The diaconate is a flexible ministry and within the Lutheran tradition deacons may or may not be ordained. The Toyenkirken project in Oslo is a remarkable example of compassionate diaconal outreach to needy people that gently brings them into contact with prayer, worship and Christian teaching. Some Protestant churches are beginning to suffer from decreasing funding for institutional *diakonia* and the salaried staff that this requires. This development can make the parochial role of deacons all the more important. From an Anglican point of view, there is considerable ambiguity in the office of deacon in some Lutheran churches. There is currently widespread debate among Lutherans about the ministry of deacons.

The Church of Norway, for example, is currently wrestling with the issue of whether deacons are within the *ministerium ecclesiasticum*, together with the pastors and bishops, or whether they are to be grouped with cantors and catechists outside the *ministerium ecclesiasticum*. Interestingly, all these ministries are commissioned or ordained by the same basic rite. The deacon is seen as having the distinct task of enabling the people of God to exercise their baptismal discipleship of prayer and care for those in need. The Church of Sweden, on the other hand, has a more clearly defined threefold ministry and its deacons are ordained – though their liturgical role tends to be rather minimal.

The Reformed tradition

Deacons have had a secure place in the Reformed tradition since John Calvin made them one of his four kinds of minister: pastors and teachers, elders and deacons. Like Luther, Calvin took the Seven appointed in Acts 6 as the prototype of deacons. The Church of Scotland, which is Presbyterian in its polity, has both male and female deacons, generally serving in either disadvantaged urban or remotely rural parishes. A liturgical role is not normally involved. The focal point of diaconal ministry in the Church of Scotland is service. The Church of Scotland is currently considering whether deacons should be ordained rather than commissioned.

The Presbyterian Church (USA) has ordained deacons who have a ministry 'to those who are in need, to the sick, to the friendless, and to any who may be in distress both within and beyond the community of faith'. But there is also a modest liturgical role. Deacons may lead the people in worship through intercession, reading the Scriptures, presenting the gifts of the people and assisting with the Lord's Supper.

The Methodist Church

The Methodist Church of Great Britain, with whom the Church of England is moving towards a new relationship through the Formal Conversations and growth in fellowship at every level of the life of the churches, has a diaconate distinct from the presbyterate. It is both an order of ministry and a religious order with a rule of life and a community ethos. The Methodist diaconate is not defined specifically as a ministry of word and sacrament. However, deacons may assist with the distribution of Holy Communion and preside at the sacrament of baptism. Although they are not required to be Local Preachers, many are and regularly preach and lead worship. Deacons work in a variety of situations: some closely linked to congregations, others in the wider community. A very small number have been 'in secular employment' (or 'other appointments'). Pastoral care, mission, teaching, encouragement and enabling can form part or all of their ministry. Methodist ministers are not first ordained deacon but are ordained directly to the presbyterate.

The Orthodox churches

In the Orthodox churches, the diaconate has a mainly liturgical role, which is regarded as essential to the liturgy. Deacons also play an important part in church administration on behalf of the bishop. The Orthodox retain the traditional threefold order and candidates for the priesthood are ordained first as deacons, though they may sometimes wait some years to be priested. The Orthodox model of an extended (though not rigidly permanent) diaconate is suggestive for our purposes.

The Anglican Communion

Within the Anglican Communion, the Episcopal Church of the USA has a considerable number of men and women deacons. They have four main roles: carriers of the sacrament, and ministers of prayer and pastoral care to the sick and housebound; providers of social care on behalf of the Church; promoters of social action, engaged with civil society; and agents of the diocesan bishop for special ministries. These roles generally go hand in hand with specific liturgical functions. The House of Bishops of ECUSA continues to be divided on the need for a transitional diaconate alongside a distinctive diaconate and on the possibility of direct ordination to the presbyterate.

The need for a distinctive diaconate is increasingly being recognized in the Anglican Church of Canada. There are also distinctive deacons in New Zealand and in one or two Australian dioceses: they are parish- and liturgy-based, even when they are working in schools or other institutions. The Church of the Province of South Africa is now committed to introducing a distinctive diaconate.

Conclusion

Altogether, this brief survey suggests that while the traditional pattern of deacons carrying social and pastoral concern beyond the bounds of the Church remains strong, a number of churches have begun to see the need to tie this into the liturgical life and pastoral oversight of the Church through ordination and a recognized role in the liturgy.

Earlier work of Faith and Order

The Faith and Order Commission of the World Council of Churches has done much to promote and collate ecumenical reflection on the nature of the ordained ministry and its role within the Church.

The Montreal Faith and Order Conference of 1963 marked a theological renewal in this area by locating ordained ministry within the ordered spiritual vitality of the whole Church. The Church is an apostolic community, animated by the Holy Spirit. Noting that there had been a widespread 'recovery of the biblical teaching about the royal priesthood of the whole people of God', it signalled the beginning of a greater ecclesiological integrity in the approach to ordained ministry. The conference recognized the ministry that belongs to the people of God *(laos)* as such, by virtue of baptism into the messianic (anointed) identity of Jesus Christ, whose body the Church is, and set the 'special ministry' of the ordained within that framework *(The Fourth World Conference on Faith and Order,* 1964, section III, pp. 61ff).

The 1964 consultation on the diaconate recognized that *diakonia* both belongs to the whole life of the Church and is concretely expressed and embodied in a particular ministry, which can serve as a sign of what the Church essentially is. Jesus Christ is the Deacon and the Church is a diaconal body. The worship *(leiturgia)* of the Church and the service *(diakonia)* of the Church need to be held together: compassionate, practical ministry to the needy has be related to the heart of the Church's life, the Eucharist. These emphases have fed into ongoing ecumenical understanding of the diaconate up to the present day.

Baptism, eucharist and ministry

A major breakthrough occurred in 1982 in the Lima document
of the Faith and Order Commission (*BEM*) – the most broadly
supported, widely endorsed and authoritative of all ecumenical texts.
BEM approaches the ecumenically sensitive question of the ordained
ministry via 'the calling of the whole people of God' and the gifts that
the Spirit gives for witness and service. Within this context, it sees the
diaconate as part of the threefold ordained ministry. The chief
responsibility of the ordained ministry is said to be 'to assemble and
build up the body of Christ by proclaiming and teaching the Word of
God, by celebrating the sacraments, and by guiding the life of the
community in its worship, its mission and its caring ministry'. On this
basis, *BEM* goes on to define the particular ministry of deacons:

> Deacons represent to the Church its calling as servant in the world. By
> struggling in Christ's name with the myriad needs of societies and persons,
> deacons exemplify the interdependence of worship and service in the
> Church's life. They exercise responsibility in the worship of the
> congregation: for example by reading the scriptures, preaching and leading
> the people in prayer. They help in the teaching of the congregation. They
> exercise a ministry of love within the community. They fulfil certain
> administrative tasks and may be elected to responsibilities for governance.
> (*BEM*, M31)

BEM marks something of a watershed in ecumenical work on the
diaconate (Brodd in *The Ministry of the Deacon*, pp. 31ff). Within *BEM*
itself, and in the process of study and reception following *BEM*, we can
discern a move away from a dominantly structural and hierarchical
approach to ordained ministry towards a more integrated ecclesiological
approach, grounding ordained ministry in the nature and mission of the
Church.

Anglican–Lutheran dialogue

Building on earlier Anglican–Lutheran dialogue and on *BEM*, *The
Niagara Report* [*Niagara*](1987) moved ecumenical theology on by
setting questions of ordained ministry, and specifically of oversight, in
the framework of the mission or apostolic commission of the Church.

Apostolicity is intrinsic to the Church and must be predicated of particular churches, whether or not they have preserved the historic threefold ministry. The *Meissen, Porvoo* and *Reuilly* agreements received impetus from this insight, as did the long-standing Lutheran–Episcopal dialogue in the USA. It suggests that some aspects of apostolicity may be present in a church, even if others are not.

While the *Meissen Agreement* (1992) between the Church of England and the Evangelical Church of Germany (EKD) – not, of course, a purely Lutheran Church – did not discuss the diaconate, it did bring about mutual acknowledgement of the apostolic authenticity of the ministries of word, sacrament and pastoral oversight *(episkope)* in the respective churches.

The *Porvoo Common Statement* [*Porvoo*] between the British and Irish Anglican Churches and Nordic and Baltic Lutheran Churches (1993), citing *BEM*, affirmed the value of the traditional threefold ministry 'as an expression of the unity we seek and also as a means for achieving it' (*Porvoo*, p. 20, para. 32j). The joint declaration, the heart of the Agreement, commits the churches 'to work towards a common understanding of diaconal ministry' (*Porvoo*, p. 58b (vii)). A brief appendix to *Porvoo*, by two Church of England participants in the dialogue, explains the background and context of diverse patterns of diaconal ministry in Anglican and Lutheran churches and draws attention to the emergence of a distinctive (non-transitional) ordained diaconate in some Anglican churches. *Porvoo* provides for the interchangeability, subject to the regulations of the participating churches, of episcopally ordained bishops, presbyters and deacons throughout the *Porvoo* communion.

The Hanover Report

Anglican (and Lutheran) reflection on the diaconate received fresh impetus through the Hanover Report of the Anglican–Lutheran International Commission *The Diaconate as Ecumenical Opportunity* (1996). For the first time in the history of bilateral ecumenical dialogue, the diaconate was the sole focus of a report. What sort of agreement would Lutherans, with their lay but commissioned diaconate as the arm of the church's social service, and Anglicans, with their ordained but mainly transitional diaconate, manage to achieve?

The Hanover Report takes the favoured ecumenical motif of *koinonia* (the New Testament Greek word translated as fellowship, communion or mutual participation) as its framework for exploring ministry. Within the matrix provided by *koinonia*, it employs the key ecclesiological themes of *diakonia* (service), *leiturgia* (worship) and *martyria* (witness) as its hermeneutical, interpretative tools (p. 10). It insists on the deacon being rooted in the ordered life of the church and its liturgy (pp. 26, 27). It advocates a renewed, distinctive, ordained diaconate with the special role of linking the needs, concerns and hopes of the world and of the Christian community with the mission, pastoral oversight and eucharistic celebration of the church (p. 51). The Hanover Report is particularly sensitive to the need for deacons not to usurp or undermine the witness, worship and service of lay people. The diaconate, the report says, should rather 'have a multiplying effect, leading others to their own specific tasks of service' (p. 56), showing the way, enabling and resourcing the ministry of the laity.

Other commitments made by the Church of England

It will already be apparent that one reason why the Church of England needs to revisit its understanding of the diaconate is in order to honour commitments that it has already made to other churches and to equip it to engage properly in future discussions to which it is also committed. In addition to the Lutheran dimension, through *Porvoo,* there are two other ecumenical partners whose theology and practice of the diaconate must be taken into account here.

One of the churches in England that has a threefold ministry is the Moravian Church. Candidates are ordained deacon but 'consecrated' presbyter or bishop. It is therefore accepted practice in the Moravian Church for deacons to preside at the Eucharist. Through the Fetter Lane Agreement (modelled on *Meissen*) the Church of England and the Moravian Church are committed to a reappraisal of the three orders of ministry, particularly the diaconate, 'in the light of the emerging ecumenical consensus and the insights of our traditions'.

The report of the informal conversations between the Methodist Church and the Church of England that led to the Formal Conversations (*Commitment to Mission and Unity,* 1996) noted that future discussions would need 'to face questions about the relationship of the three orders of ministry to each other within the basic oneness of the ordained ministry', and it particularly highlighted, in this context, the nature and role of the diaconate (para. 20). It is likely that the report of the Formal Conversations will note the differences in the theology and practice of the diaconate between the two churches.

The report of the Anglican–Methodist International Commission *Sharing in the Apostolic Communion* (1996) points out that *diakonia* in the sense of servanthood is the mark of all ordained ministry, whether that of bishop, presbyter or deacon. However, this dimension of the Church's ministry is particularly expressed in the office of deacon which 'sets forth the essential sign of Christ's work and purpose for the world (Mark 10.35-45)'. The servant ministry of the deacon has liturgical, pastoral and proclamatory aspects. It is exercised 'both within the body of believers and more broadly in the world ... It is a distinctive and lifelong ministry. It is traditionally closely associated with the work of the bishop.' Bishops have 'a special collaborative link with the deacons' (50, 51, 53). The reception of this report, among both Anglicans and Methodists, may have consequences for both churches' understanding of the diaconate.

Summary of ecumenical aspects

A more consistently ecclesiological approach to ordained ministry has characterized ecumenical reflection since *BEM*. This approach has helped to foster recognition of the assured place of the diaconate within a diversified ordained ministry. It has encouraged us to see each order of ministry as having its distinctive commission, though without pretending that the set of tasks assigned to any particular order is completely exclusive. It has affirmed the dependence of all ministry on the empowering of the Holy Spirit, and generated an increasing awareness that the deacon is meant to be a bridge between the liturgical and pastoral work of the church, between the Eucharist and the workaday world, between the bishop as chief pastor and father in God and the flock of Christ entrusted to his care. This growing ecumenical consensus about the place of the ordained ministry – and in particular of the diaconate – in the ordered life of the Body of Christ has been accompanied by widespread calls for a renewal of the diaconate and recognition of its distinctive role. Why is this? What factors have contributed to the diaconate coming under the spotlight?

chapter 4

Social change and the mission imperative

It is widely recognized that in the period of late modernity (sometimes called postmodernity) the accepted, traditional structures of society – structures of class, wealth, settlement, career stability – have been dissolving. Fragmentation rather than coherence, fluidity rather than stability, have become significant features of Western societies. As a result, the life of community is at a premium. While the values of true community are extolled by politicians, political thinkers and church leaders, the reality is experienced as elusive and even illusory by many people. Traditional, relatively stable patterns of community, based on settlement, division of labour and social deference, have given way, to a considerable extent, to various unstable and ephemeral congeries of individuals and groups. Social relationships are increasingly based on networks of work and leisure association, career paths and hobbies, as much as on extended family, place and role. Moral communities, grounded in a shared tradition and common values that transcend self-interest, have been giving way to 'lifestyle enclaves'. Society is experiencing a lack of coherence and connectedness. The sense of the common good is felt to be threatened. In this situation there is an obvious need for focal, representative people and focal, representative structures that can bring individuals, families and communities together. How does this situation relate to the churches and their mission?

The Christian churches – and especially churches with a nationwide ministry and a recognized role and voice in the articulation of public doctrine, such as the Church of England – are wedded, for historical and ecclesiological reasons, to a dispersed form of mission: territorial, settlement-based, geographically distributed. This has been the strength of the Church of England and still forms the backbone of its mission in the nation. The parochial structure, under episcopal oversight, provides the framework for the delivery of a ministry of word, sacrament and pastoral care. It ensures access to the ministrations of the Church and at the same time defines the necessary scope and salutary limits for pastoral responsibility.

This territorial ministry is substantially supplemented by various forms of sector ministry, through chaplaincies to industry and commerce, to educational, penal and welfare institutions and to the armed services. This extensive and variegated sector ministry forms an integral and vital part of the Church of England's mission within the nation and to all its people and is becoming increasingly important to the Church's mission in a fragmented and mobile society.

In the Anglican tradition the Church's mission tends to be conceived in broadly pastoral terms, embracing the ministry of word and sacrament as an aspect of the cure (or care) of souls in a community. Mission in its broadest sense is not something other than, or separate from the attractive power of the life of communion within the Body of Christ, sustained by the means of grace (chiefly word and sacrament) and shepherded by pastors who share the bishop's oversight. That life of communion proclaims the gospel in word and deed and thus carries forward the mission entrusted to the Church.

Deacons in mission

However, there remains a substantial gap between the worship and fellowship of the Church, centred on its ministry of word, sacrament and pastoral care and oversight, on the one hand, and large numbers of people in our society whose contact with the Church is tenuous or negligible. The factors that make up the phenomenon of 'secularization' have weakened the public profile of the churches and their impact within the community.

In their mission strategy, the churches have focused on the problem of how to bridge this gap. While much short-term evangelism has been geared to persuading people to come to Church (not at all an unworthy aim in itself, of course), deeper reflection on mission has concentrated on ways in which the church can reach out to meet people and their needs where they are, but without compromising the Church's

21

God-given identity as the Body of Christ or diluting its unique message, the Christian gospel. The apostolicity (i.e. 'sentness') of the Church must inform its approach to mission.

In recent ecumenical reflection on the diaconate, as we have already mentioned, the ministry of deacons has been seen as that of a go-between, a bridge, an envoy, whose special ministry is to take the message, meaning and values of the liturgy, as a key expression of the gospel, into the heart of the world and, by the same token, to bring the needs and cares of the world into the heart of the Church's worship and fellowship. Deacons have been seen as those who, grounded in the teaching and worship of the Body of Christ, carry the good news, in word and sacrament, and through compassionate service, to those whom Christ came to seek and to save.

Of course deacons alone cannot 'bridge the gap'. They cannot carry the whole burden of the Church's mission. Their role is not to attempt to do everything themselves, but primarily to enable the people of God to carry out their baptismal responsibilities of prayer and compassionate service – encouraging, resourcing, organizing and overseeing this on behalf of the bishop and the parish priest. Deacons can only be effective in mission when the worshipping community in which they are based is committed to a missionary vision.

Moreover, deacons are not the only ones to have a 'go-between' ministry. Their ministry should not in any way detract from the proper ministry of bishops and presbyters, who also have a 'bridge' ministry themselves. Readers too can make effective connections between Church and world. Nor should deacons be expected to compensate for deficiencies elsewhere. A renewed diaconate is not a panacea for all the weaknesses of the Church in mission. Deacons take their place alongside the witness and service of lay people and of other ordained ministers, presbyters and bishops.

Distinctive but not exclusive

All Christians are 'sent' or 'apostled' by the Lord for witness and service in the world, according to their particular calling. Every pastor is called to engage in mission – not least the bishop, who, according to the

Ordinal, is called to lead the diocese in its mission. But each one, whether lay or ordained, fulfils the mission imperative in his or her special way within the economy of salvation, the sharing and distribution of gifts and callings within the Body of Christ.

The Church lives solely from the life of communion *(koinonia)* of the Holy Trinity and by the grace of God is enabled – albeit utterly inadequately – to reflect it sacramentally in its own experience of fellowship *(koinonia)*. Among the Persons of the Holy Trinity there is no difference of value, so to speak, but there are distinctions of role or relationship that belong to the divine order. This subtle understanding of distinction-in-communion is reflected in the doctrine of holy order in the ministry of the Church. 'A trinitarian theology of the Church will speak of the oneness of the Church not as a homogeneous unity, but as a differentiated oneness of distinctive persons-in-relation who discover their particularity in active relationships of giving and receiving' *(Eucharistic Presidency*, 1997, 2.25). In the light of a trinitarian ecclesiology, the ministry of deacons – like that of presbyters and bishops, for that matter – can be seen to be distinctive without being completely exclusive.

In the context of social change, a renewed diaconate may particularly embody, within the ordered life of the Body of Christ, the aspect of 'reaching out', making connections, building bridges, consolidating community and putting the treasures of the gospel at the service of human need.

In times of crisis

In the past couple of decades, perhaps as a result of rapid social and political change in Europe, there seems to have been a remarkable increase in the demand for pastoral support, especially in times of crisis. Tragic national events, and more local natural or man-made disasters, when the whole nation grieves, seem to produce a call for help in making sense of lives that have been so cruelly curtailed. The clergy, as the publicly identifiable representatives of the Church, respond with dedication and skill to the pastoral demands that these situations place upon them. However, the demand for counselling support for those caught up in such disasters is so great that at present it can often only be met by 'secular' counsellors.

The Scandinavian national churches, with whom we are in communion through the Porvoo Agreement, have recently experienced the same phenomenon, perhaps even more intensely. The *Estonia* ferry disaster and more domestic tragedies, such as major fires, have brought home to the Church authorities in such countries as Sweden, the huge demand for pastoral ministry at such moments and in ongoing support thereafter. The Church of Sweden takes this aspect of its mission so seriously that it has national or central arrangements in place to coordinate and resource the pastoral response of bishops, clergy and laity in such circumstances. (The Church of England, numerically larger and with many more dioceses than the Church of Sweden, has regionally based contingency plans, many of which are coordinated ecumenically, for responding to emergencies and its Board for Social Responsibility has produced 'Guidelines for Faith Communities when Dealing with Disasters' 1997.)

These factors have suggested to some of our Scandinavian colleagues that the diaconate is indeed needed more than ever, as a ministry of word, sacrament and pastoral care, responding to the spiritual hunger and pastoral needs of many in the community who still look first to the Church, even though they may not attend church services very often. Is there not a corresponding pastoral need in this country that could be met particularly by some deacons (though not only by them: also by other clergy and qualified lay people), especially trained in pastoral counselling, accustomed to dealing with bereavements of various kinds and firmly rooted in theology and worship? It is true to say – and well worth underlining here – that the principal motive behind the ecumenical rediscovery of the diaconate has been pastoral and missiological.

chapter 5

Renewal in the theology of ministry, lay and ordained

Through sustained theological dialogue, both multilateral and bilateral, and many experiences of local, practical cooperation, the churches have come to understand each other better during the past half-century. The ecumenical movement has succeeded in transcending, to some extent, the inherited stereotypes that the churches have had of each other and in overcoming some major oppositions in doctrine. One of the most salient areas of progress is that of the theology of Christian ministry. Here the notion of representative ministry has proved particularly helpful in fostering consensus (for what follows see *Eucharistic Presidency*, 1997 and *Bishops in Communion*, 2000).

Royal priesthood and representative ministry

As we have seen, a major concern, in the ecumenical renewal of the diaconate, has been to help to bridge the gulf opened up by the process of secularization between the Church's life of communion *(koinonia)* and the needs of the wider community in which it is set. The idea of representative ministry is fundamentally relational. The ministry is seen as representative of both Christ and the Church – of Christ in and through his Body. The theme of representativeness brings ministry into close relationship with community. 'The responsibility of certain people to act for all is rooted in a sense of relationship between them and the community' *(Eucharistic Presidency*, 1997, 1.40).

To represent Christ and his Church through a ministry of word, sacrament and pastoral care requires authorization (the giving or sharing of authority) from those one represents. This authority is given in ordination when a person is commissioned and empowered in the name of God. In licensing, the authorization is channelled to a particular portion of the people of God.

Clearly, in the Church, the authority for public ministry comes not simply from the community but from the Lord as Head of the Church. The Head cannot be separated from the members of the Body. Together, as St Augustine of Hippo says, they comprise the whole Christ *(totus Christus)*.

Ecumenical ecclesiology tends to begin from the calling of the people of God into existence through faith and baptism. 1 Peter 2 uses cumulative imagery from the Hebrew Bible, our Old Testament, to show the high calling of all Christians: from corner stone to temple, from temple to priesthood and from priesthood to sacrifice. 'Come to him, a living stone, though rejected by mortals yet chosen and precious in God's sight, and like living stones, let yourselves be built into a spiritual house, to be a holy priesthood, to offer spiritual sacrifices acceptable to God through Jesus Christ.' Sharing in Christ's messianic identity as our great Prophet, Priest and King, Christians are incorporated into God's purpose for Israel.

Invoking the familiar imagery of baptism, as a passage from darkness to light (as well as from death to life), 1 Peter affirms that baptized believers belong to the corporate priesthood of the Church that is both kingly and prophetic: '... you are a chosen race, a royal priesthood, a holy nation, God's own people, in order that you may proclaim the mighty acts of him who called you out of darkness into his marvellous light' (1 Peter 2.9f). As a royal house, Christians play their part in the governance of Christ's kingdom. As a priestly nation, they offer spiritual sacrifices to God through Christ, above all the offering of their very selves (Romans 12.1). As a prophetic people, they make known the saving work of God in Christ. The *laos* comprises the whole people of God collectively, and is theologically prior to the distinction between 'laity' and 'clergy'. Ordination does not take anyone out of the *laos*.

There is wide agreement that all Christians, through faith and baptism, through witness and daily discipleship, represent Christ to their neighbour (see the House of Bishops' statement *Bishops in Communion*,

2000). For the dedicated Christian, all that he or she does is done in the name of Christ and consecrated to the glory of God (Colossians 3.17; Ephesians 5.20). Christians are Christ-bearers. The whole Church is sent by Christ into the world and is therefore said to be apostolic, from the Greek verb to send. The idea of representation therefore applies to all Christians, not simply to the ordained (though it does apply in a particular way to them). Representativeness is differentiated in various ministries and it is the differentiation of the diaconate that particularly needs to be clarified.

There is also an ecumenical consensus that a ministry recognized by the Church is not by any means confined to the ordained. All Christians have received a spiritual gift or charism through baptism (1 Corinthians 12.4-7,13). Every single limb or organ of the Body of Christ has a vital role for the sake of the well-being of the whole body (1 Corinthians 12.12-27). All are called to serve, that is to say, to minister in one way or another. When that ministry is called forth by the community, recognized and owned by the community, in both tacit and implicit as well as explicit and formal ways, individuals are seen to act in the name of Christ and his Church.

It is vital to affirm that every baptized believer is called to ministry in one way or another. However, this is not a matter of individual whim, or staking a personal claim, but is subject to the sovereign call of the Holy Spirit, which the Church is called and equipped to discern. Ministry is something more than Christian discipleship. The two ideas are, of course, closely connected but not identical. Discipleship embraces all that we think, say or do. It is not necessarily public, representative or formally accountable. Ministry, however, is a form of service that is representative of Christ and the Church in a way that is publicly acknowledged and publicly accountable, either explicitly or tacitly.

In the case of authorized ministers, both lay (Readers, Churchwardens) and ordained (deacons, priests), that public acknowledgement and accountability is subject to the oversight of the bishop. The Canons of the Church of England describe the bishop as 'the chief pastor of all that are within his diocese, as well laity as clergy, and their father in God' (Canon C 18). The bishop shares his ministry of oversight, with its responsibility for the ministry of the word and the administration of the sacraments, with the parish priest in a cure (or care) of souls that is 'both yours and mine'. Both bishop and presbyter are assisted by the deacon as a representative minister of word, sacrament and pastoral care.

Ordained ministry

Building on the representative nature of all public ministry in the Church, whether lay or ordained, there is broad ecumenical agreement that there is a need for ministries that are given authority to speak and act in a public, representative way that goes beyond what lay people are authorized to do. Of course, all recognized ministry, whether lay or ordained, is the ministry of Christ. The ordained, however, minister in the name of Christ and with his authority in a publicly representative way. Ordained ministers are called, trained, commissioned, licensed and accountable to higher authority in a particular way. They are set apart for diaconal, presbyteral or episcopal ministry for life. Their ministry – the ministry of the word, the administration of the sacraments and the exercise of pastoral care and oversight in the Church – is carried out in ways that are laid down in the law of the church and overseen through the government of the church, that is to say, by means of structures of synodical conciliarity and episcopal collegiality. Because the ordained do not exercise their ministry in their own name but in Christ's name and by his commission and authority (Article XXVI), their ministry represents, stands for and typifies the ministry of Christ through his Body the Church.

Some important ecumenical agreed texts have affirmed this broad understanding of the particular representative calling of the ordained within the overall understanding of the calling and ministry of the *laos* or people of God. They affirm an apostolic ministry as well as an apostolic community.

BEM (the multilateral Lima report of 1982) states: 'In order to fulfil its mission, the Church needs persons who are publicly and continually responsible for pointing to its fundamental dependence on Jesus Christ, and thereby provide, within a multiplicity of gifts, a focus of its unity.' *BEM* adds: 'The ministry of such persons, who since very early times have been ordained, is constitutive for the life and witness of the Church' (*BEM*, M8). On this point, Anglicans, Orthodox and Roman Catholics, Lutherans, Reformed and Methodists are agreed.

The report of the Anglican–Reformed international dialogue *God's Reign and our Unity* (1984) says: 'Ordination involves as part of its essential nature the entrusting of authority to the ordained person to act focally and representatively for the whole Church' (GROU 86).

The Hanover Report *The Diaconate as Ecumenical Opportunity* (1996) notes that 'there are some offices in the church which enact and bring into focus central aspects of the mission of the entire Church and also form the identity of the person involved' (p. 25).

The statement on ministry and ordination, agreed in 1973, of the Anglican–Roman Catholic International Commission (ARCIC) is slightly more expansive. ARCIC states that 'the goal of the ordained ministry is to serve [the] priesthood of all the faithful'. It continues: 'Like any human community the Church requires a focus of leadership and unity, which the Holy Spirit provides in the ordained ministry' (ARCIC, *The Final Report*, p. 33: Ministry and Ordination 7). With regard to the threefold ministry, ARCIC goes on to affirm that:

> an essential element in the ordained ministry is its responsibility for oversight *(episcope)* ... Presbyters are joined with the bishop in his oversight of the church and in the ministry of the word and the sacraments; they are given authority to preside at the eucharist and to pronounce absolution. Deacons, though not so empowered, are associated with bishops and presbyters in the ministry of word and sacrament, and assist in oversight. *(Ibid.,* pp. 33f: Ministry and Ordination 9).

The statement of the House of Bishops on *Eucharistic Presidency* (1997) refines the language of representation. Noting some ambiguity about the common metaphor 'focus' as applied to the ordained ministry, it suggests that the ordained ministry is given rather 'to promote, release and clarify' the ministry of the whole Church and to exemplify and sustain the four credal marks or dimensions of the Church: one, holy, catholic and apostolic (3.26). Of course, a focus does precisely both clarify and illuminate.

Christ and the Spirit in Church and world

Undergirding the renewal of the theology of ministry is a Christological renewal of ecclesiology. The Church is rightly seen, not merely as an institution, with a chequered history and with structures that can be analysed by sociological methods, though it is inevitably at least this. It can be rediscovered as the agent, organ or sacrament (in the Prayer Book Catechism's sense of 'an outward and visible sign of an inward and spiritual grace') of Christ's presence and activity in the world through the power of the Holy Spirit. For all its imperfections and need of continual reform and renewal, the Church is recognized in ecumenical theology as a sign, instrument and foretaste – in other words, a kind of sacrament – of the fulfilment of God's good purposes for the creation.

A Christological approach to the Church necessarily involves a Christological approach to the Church's ministry. The primary ministry is that of Jesus Christ himself. All Christian ministry is a participation in his. Clearly, on this premise, there cannot be any expression of ministry that is other than the ministry of Jesus Christ in his Body through the power of the Holy Spirit (GROU 74; *Eucharistic Presidency*, 1997, 3.6). All ministry, whether ordained or lay, is therefore a channel of the risen Christ's ongoing work in the world. The threefold ordained ministry, as 'an outward and visible sign' of the working of divine grace through the Church, has a sacramental significance. Holy order may be seen as a 'sacramental sign' of Christ's ministry in and through his Body.

The Incarnation, with its self-emptying and self-offering for the sake of those God loved in Christ, is the model of all Christian ministry. As the Bishop of Salisbury suggested in the General Synod debate that commissioned this report, coming to be with us, sharing in our condition, engaging with our dilemmas are the hallmarks of incarnational ministry, Christ's and ours (General Synod, *Report of Proceedings*, 1998, p. 73). A renewed, distinctive diaconate, operating as a catalyst for Christian discipleship, in the mission space between worship and the world, can help the Church to become more incarnational. In worship the Church gathers to receive and to celebrate its identity, to be renewed in the Spirit, and to be sent forth in the name of Christ and in the power of the same Spirit to bring God's reconciling, healing grace to a world full of brokenness. We have not been good at doing equal justice to these two vital movements of the Church's life: sending and gathering. The re-envisioned diaconate can help to hold them together.

Rediscovery of the biblical idea of *diakonia*

Not the least of the reasons why reconsideration of the office of deacon is timely is that recent biblical scholarship has shed new light on the original meaning of the key New Testament Greek words and of the ideas that lie behind them. The richness and subtlety of the Greek is often obscured in translation. The nearest English equivalents are frequently blunt instruments to convey the sense of Scripture.

Fresh interpretation

This is not the place to attempt a substantive account of recent developments in the interpretation of the text, which have arisen largely from the pioneering work of the Australian scholar John N. Collins (1990). These fresh scholarly findings were fully recognized in the debate in the General Synod that established this working party. Although the argument of this report is not dependent on etymology that can always be contested, but rests on broad theological, canonical and missiological premises, these findings have major implications for our understanding of the 'diaconal' aspect of the Church's mission and for the office of deacon in particular.

These important developments in New Testament interpretation entered the public domain soon after the report of 1988 *Deacons in the Ministry of the Church* was published. That report was still inevitably working with the received understanding of *diakonia* as service, even humble service. According to the report, diaconal ministry is the 'serving, self-giving aspect of the Church's ministry' (p. 78: para. 241). The emphasis is on the self-emptying, suffering character of Christ's own ministry (p. 79: para. 247). Though other nuances are acknowledged, the report is clear that the content of *diakonia* is service and that the translation of *diakonos* is simply 'servant' in an unqualified sense (p. 81:253).

Of course, the self-emptying humility of the Son of God, evoked by St Paul in Philippians 2, is the benchmark for Christian attitudes and behaviour. The ideal of service remains fundamental. We should not react so far against the received interpretation that we lose sight of the servant character of all Christian ministry. That is still crucial to the understanding of *diakonia*. But, since 1988, a wealth of meaning has been discovered that heavily qualifies the approach of the earlier report.

The inherited understanding of *diakoneo* in 1988, when *Deacons in the Ministry of the Church* was published, meant 'to serve or wait at table'. Eduard Schweizer reflects what many others have written when he writes in *Church Order in the New Testament*:

> In the development of Greek the basic meaning, 'to serve at table', was extended to include the comprehensive idea of 'serving'. It nearly always denotes something of inferior value. (Schweizer, 1961, p. 174f)

John N. Collins in *Diakonia: Re-interpreting the Ancient Sources* (1990) explored the meaning of *diakonia* in secular usage and then applied it to the New Testament references. He came to the conclusion that the primary meaning centred around message, agency and attendance.

- As bearer of a message, a *diakonos* is a spokesperson, an envoy, a courier, a go-between, who is entrusted with important tidings.

- In terms of agency, a *diakonos* is an ambassador, a mediator, a person who is given a commission to carry out a task and to act on behalf of someone in authority.

- In terms of attendance, *diakonia* is attendance upon a person or within a household, on whose behalf one performs various tasks (not merely a servant who waits at table).

The crucial point is that, in classical Greek usage, the *diakonia/diakonos* group of words refer to responsible agency on behalf of a person in authority and involve the fulfilling of a vital task. These Greek terms certainly do not have connotations of inferiority or of menial service.

This fundamental meaning is carried through into New Testament usage. The central sense is to do with responsible agency and an authoritative commission. The Apostles themselves are entrusted with a *diakonia* or ministry (Acts 1.17; 6.4; 20.24) which stems from the Lord's commission to carry the good news into the world. St Paul refers to himself as *diakonos* in the sense of an instrument of Christ to bring others to faith in him (1 Corinthians 3.5). In upholding his authority against his detractors, St Paul insists that he is truly a *diakonos* with the Lord's commission, a minister of the new covenant in the power of the Spirit (2 Corinthians 3.6; 6.4; 11.23). The New Testament word for servant or slave is not *diakonos* but (usually) *doulos*. There are two specific texts which provide a focus for these new emphases.

Mark 10.45
This verse has been used as a scriptural reading at many ordination services: 'For the Son of Man came not to be served *(diakonethenai)* but to serve *(diakonesai)*, and to give his life a ransom for many.' If the verb from the *diakonos* family of words means the carrying out of a task either established by God, or by the authority of an Apostle or another authority within the community, then in simple terms it means: 'For the Son of Man is not one who has attendants whom he can summon or despatch, but is one who was sent by God with the task of dying to provide a ransom for many.' Such an interpretation is in keeping with the emphasis that, early in the second century, St Ignatius of Antioch, on his way to be martyred in Rome instructed the Trallians:

> Correspondingly, every one must show the deacon respect. They represent Jesus Christ, just as the bishop has the role of the Father and the presbyters are like God's council and an apostolic band. You cannot have a Church without these. (Trallians 3)

For Ignatius the deacon is part of the local hierarchy and is almost inseparable from the bishop and presbyters.

In Mark 10.45 Jesus comes close to being the deacon of the Father, the one who carries out the Father's will which for him is to go to Jerusalem and there to give his life as a ransom for many.

Luke 22.24-30
This passage deals with the dispute about greatness that follows directly after the account of the institution of the Lord's Supper. 'For who is greater, the one who is at the table or the one who serves *(diakonōn)*? Is it not the one at the table? But I am among you as one who serves *(diakonōn)* [Luke 22.27]'. The presupposition behind this pericope is a world that is so ordered that there are those who lord it over others, who exercise authority and who are waited upon. The presupposition is that the one who lies at table is greater than the one who attends at table. So Turid Karlsen Seim writes:

> *diakonōn* is proposed as the honorific designation. The inversion of the role-expectations in these verses does not, however, mean that the roles themselves are abolished, nor does it imply a clear reversal. The leaders

remain leaders, but the new ideals for their leadership are established. It is
not that the servants are now to rule, but those who rule are to be as the
diakonos. (*The Double Message*, 1994, p. 85)

Despite what some commentators have claimed, Jesus is not the waiter,
rather he shows the disciples that while leaders remain leaders they are
to lead as those who serve. So the authority of Jesus brings together in
paradoxical form two traditional roles, those of servant and ruler. He
bequeaths to the Church the ideal of servant leadership.

These new insights provide the Church with categories which can apply
to the ordained ministry – a flexible concept that embodies being
commissioned by God or the Church to carry out a task or to convey a
message; a concept that does not lose the caritative content, but sets it
within a pattern of leadership that enables, as subsequently can be seen,
the whole People of God to carry out their baptismal responsibility.

The transition in New Testament times from this general sense of
authoritative commissioning for service to the distinctive ministry of
those called deacons is not clear. However, deacons *(diakonois)* are
specifically mentioned as a separate 'order' of ministry, along with
overseers *(episkopois)*, in Philippians 1.1 and 1 Timothy 3.1-13. Women
deacons may well be mentioned in Romans 16.1 (Phoebe) and in 1
Timothy 3.11. Associated with overseers, deacons clearly have a
respected and defined role in the Christian community. The historic
connection between deacons and their bishop – first found implicitly in
St Ignatius of Antioch – can be traced back to this New Testament link
between *diakonois* and *episkopois*.

Key biblical words

Diakonia takes its place in a pattern of New Testament Christological
images. Three key Greek terms help to elucidate the work of Christ in
the world through the Church: *martyria*, witness; *leitourgia*, worship;
and *diakonia*, service (cf. *The Diaconate as Ecumenical Opportunity*,
passim). Each of these dimensions of the Church's life is grounded
biblically in the person and work of Jesus Christ:

Martyria
Jesus Christ is the paradigm of witness. He is the proto-martyr. He is the
faithful witness, the witness unto death. He testifies by his life, ministry,

death and resurrection to the gospel of God's saving love for the world. Because he is, in his person and work, the content and substance of the gospel, he is able to receive the testimony of God to his mission while himself ascribing all glory to the Father (John 3.11; 8.54f; 17.5,26; Romans 1.3f; Revelation 1.5).

Leitourgia

Jesus Christ is the paradigm of worship. He is the one Priest in whom all priesthood is included. His whole existence, in terms of both his active and his passive obedience, is a self-oblation to the Father, offered in filial love. As our great high priest in heaven, he ever lives to intercede for us. For our part, we offer our worship and service only in and through him. In the Eucharist our own unworthy sacrifice is gathered up in the continual, perfect movement of his self-offering that is there commemorated and celebrated (Mark 1.11; John 14.31; 17.4; 1 Corinthians 10.16-18; Hebrews 13.15, etc.; Romans 12.1).

Diakonia

Jesus Christ is the paradigm of obedience to the will of God. He is the great Deacon, the one who is among us as one who serves (Luke 22.27). He is the suffering servant of the Lord, sent into the world with a divine commission. The service of God involves the service of his people. In his own life Jesus authorizes a pattern for his disciples of sacrificial love to each other and to other needy folk. His leadership takes the form of sacrificial love, meeting the real needs of others. This emphasis on self-giving sacrificial love, that is the dominant idea in earlier understandings of diaconal ministry, remains valid; it must not be lost sight of when we look for a renewed diaconate. Service in Christ is true greatness and to be great is to be a servant. The servant bears his or her master's commission and carries out the task assigned (Mark 10.41-5). But in the biblical paradigm the servant is also vindicated and exalted. The servant has God's authority and represents the people. Yet he suffers and sacrifices himself before he is vindicated and given glory (Isaiah 53.12; cf. Philippians 2.1-11) – showing us that service in the name of Christ is neither menial nor servile.

Fresh application

Recent insights of biblical interpretation enable us to see the office of deacon in a new light. The deacon is an instrument of God's purpose, of the Kingdom of God. The deacon is invested with authority by Christ through the Church, in the person of the bishop. The deacon is not set apart for menial service, is not expected to exhibit humility more than others, and is not called to bear more than his or her fair share of suffering for Christ's sake. All Christians are called to present themselves as a living sacrifice in God's service for Christ's sake (Romans 12.1).

The deacon is a person on a mission, a messenger or ambassador, making connections, building bridges, faithfully delivering his or her mandate. As such, the deacon says something about the nature of the Church as Christ's Body, becoming indeed a sign of what the Church is called to be. The Church is at its most visible when it is exercising its *diakonia*, its commissioned service in the world. Deacons can be understood as the persons who represent to the Church, and therefore to the world, its authoritative calling as the servant of God and God's people (a service that takes many forms, including liturgical and proclamatory ones). In the language of *Eucharistic Presidency* (1997) their office, like that of all the ordained, is to promote, release and clarify the nature of the Church. Deacons do this in relation to the *diakonia* of the Church as they model, encourage and coordinate the diaconal ministry of the people of God.

A deacon may be regarded, therefore, as an ecclesial sign, embodying a truth about the whole Church and about all its ministries. In ordination the deacon receives a particular ecclesial identity before God through the Church. That identity relates to the Kingdom of God that has dawned in Jesus Christ but remains to be fulfilled, and to the place and role of the Christian Church in God's coming kingly reign. Christ is himself the embodiment of the Kingdom (*autobasileia*). But he is also the archetypal baptized one, as well as the archetypal Deacon, Priest and Bishop. In himself he holds together Kingdom, Church and ministry.

This particular ecclesial identity is, however, true of the Church as a whole and of all her ministries. It is true of presbyters and bishops as well as of deacons. All three orders are given to embody in a visible, public and representative way what is true of the Church as such. In ordaining men and women, the Church is witnessing in a concrete way to how it understands its God-given mission. Presbyters and bishops have ministries that, while they are distinctive, overlap in various ways, both with each other and with the ministry of the deacon. The three orders of ordained ministry overlap also with the ministry of lay people. This is inevitable because the work entrusted to the Church is an integrated whole, not a random assortment of discrete functions. All according to their vocation and ministry play their part. The orders of ministry are distinctive without being exclusive. The doctrine of the Holy Trinity, with its differentiation of persons in unity of being, is our paradigm here. The three orders focus constituent aspects of the Church.

There is something embodied in the diaconate that serves to hold this diversity of ministerial calling and task together. The diaconate (like the presbyterate and the episcopate) not only reflects what is true of the *laos* (that is to say, of all Christians); but it is also the *sine qua non* of all ordained ministry, the base line, the template on which it is fashioned. All Christian ministry, ordained or lay, is grounded in *diakonia* because it is all dependent on the fundamental divine commission of the Church in the service of the Kingdom. Therefore all ministry is commissioned to have that connecting, bridging, role, reaching out in the name of Christ, whatever else it may be called to be and to do. But this fundamental divine commission for the service of God and God's people is visibly, sacramentally expressed in the order of deacon.

Our approach, that regards the diaconate as somehow fundamental to all ordained ministry, seems to be fully in keeping with the normative 1662 Ordinal and the Canons which require that ordination to the diaconate shall normally precede, by a minimum of one year, ordination to the presbyterate (Canon C 3. 7, 8). And as Canon C 1. 2 says: 'No person who has been admitted to the order of bishop, priest, or deacon can ever be divested of the character of his order.' The rule that a bishop cannot be divested of the character of the priesthood, and bishop and priest cannot be divested of the character of the diaconate, suggests that the prior ordination somehow remains integral to the subsequent ordination. This principle seems to reflect the interrelatedness of the more functional precursors of our present orders of ministry in the New Testament. In Scripture there is a close relationship between elders *(presbuteroi)* and overseers *(episkopoi)* (Acts 20,17,28; Titus 1.5,7), just as there is between overseers and deacons (Philippians 1.1).
1 Timothy, on the other hand, refers to deacons, presbyters and overseers (1 Timothy 3.1,8; 5.1,17,19).

We may say that a priest cannot be a priest, dedicated to declaring and celebrating the reconciling work of Christ that releases God's blessing for God's creation, unless he or she is in the first place a deacon – commissioned and empowered for the service of God. A bishop cannot be a bishop, entrusted with oversight *(episkope)* of the Church's life in relation to its unity, holiness, catholicity and apostolicity, unless he is in the first place a deacon – commissioned and empowered for the service of God – and a priest – dedicated to serve God's purpose of reconciliation in Christ. That is presumably why bishops have sometimes worn the deacon's vestment, the dalmatic, as well as the priest's vestments, the alb, stole and chasuble. All ministry derives from Jesus Christ who is at once Deacon (Mark 10.45), Priest (Hebrews 4.14–) and Bishop (1 Peter 2.25: *episkopos*). Our ministry, whether lay or ordained, is no more and no less than a participation in his.

chapter 6

The renewed diaconate and recent developments in lay and ordained ministry

We must now ask how this rediscovered insight affects the diaconate's relation to the laity and to lay ministry. The motion, carried in an amended form, that set up this working party committed it to be 'mindful of the changing patterns of ministry within the Church of England since the diaconate was last considered'. In addressing these changing patterns, we will take into account the burgeoning of Reader ministry, the emergence of Lay Parish (or Pastoral) Assistants and the move towards Local Ministry Teams. We need to ask how a renewed or permanent diaconate would relate to these flourishing ministries. We will also consider the relation of a renewed diaconate to Ordained Local Ministry. Finally, we will refer to the desire of a constituency of the Church of England to see a permanent 'non-headship' ministry available to women. In focusing on these aspects, we do not overlook the fact that other recognized lay ministers within the Church of England – especially those of Church Army Evangelists and Accredited Lay Workers – have strong diaconal characteristics.

Distinctive deacons and recognized lay ministries

Readers

Of course, the ministry of Reader is not a recent development. The office of Reader is attested in the early Church. By the beginning of the third century, Readers expounded the Scriptures and preached and were, therefore, well qualified intellectually. By the fifth century, Readers had become members of a Minor Order and had lost much of their distinctive ministry. In the English Reformation the Minor Orders were abolished, but the office of Reader was revived as a lay office under Elizabeth I by Archbishop Parker in 1561. Readers ministered in poorly endowed parishes where there was no incumbent. They were permitted to read Morning and Evening Prayer but not to preach. They were allowed to bury the dead and conduct the Churching of Women following childbirth. They had therefore a pastoral function but no sacramental role. Readers were never very numerous, but there is evidence that the office continued to be exercised in parts of the North of England until the mid-eighteenth century.

It is the flourishing of Reader ministry in the Church of England that is a comparatively recent development. The revival of Reader ministry stems from the decision of the archbishops and bishops of the Church of England, meeting at Lambeth Palace on Ascension Day 1866, to adopt the decision of the Convocation of Canterbury to reinstate the office of Reader. The episcopate resolved that Readership would be a lay office, to which candidates would be admitted by prayer and delivery of the New Testament, but without the laying on of hands. The bishop could revoke the office at his discretion. The commission of the bishop would authorize the Reader 'to render general aid to the clergy in all ministrations not strictly requiring the aid of one in Holy Orders; to read the Lessons in church; to read prayers and Holy Scripture, and to explain the same in such places as the bishop's commission shall define'.

Readers of course no longer have a monopoly among lay people of reading the lessons in church, though they may still have a special liturgical role in reading the Epistle or Gospel. Though other lay people may be authorized by the bishop to preach on occasion, Readers preach by virtue of their office, under the direction of the incumbent. They administer the Holy Communion *ex officio* and not by special episcopal permission. They may be given the bishop's permission to conduct funerals (granted the goodwill of the bereaved family in each case). Many Readers assist in pastoral ministry within the parish, as provided for by Canon E 4.

Readers comprise an important resource for the Church's work today. Their numbers are buoyant, their training is thorough (and nationally monitored), their oversight is rigorous. There are now more Readers than there are stipendiary parochial clergy (about 10,000). Readers are qualified and commissioned to work closely with the clergy and to assist them in the work of the ministry. Though the core ministry of Readers is liturgical and homiletical, their commission is versatile. With close support and encouragement from the parochial clergy, active recognition by the diocesan bishop, and adequate continuing ministerial education, Readers are well placed to continue to make a sustained contribution to the Church's ministry and mission.

It is true that Readers may, with specific permission, carry out all the duties assigned to deacons, with the not insignificant exceptions of baptism (although in an emergency, anyone 'doing what the Church does' may baptize) and officiating at marriages. Readers belong within the representative (publicly acknowledged and accountable) ministry of the Church. Yet their ministry remains a lay one. Reader ministry is an office rather than an order. Though it is nationally recognized and is significant of the ministry that belongs to the whole people of God, the office of Reader is not an 'ecclesial sign' in the same way that the ordained ministry is. It is not irrevocable like the orders of deacons, priests and bishops. Holy order is regarded by the Church as 'a sacramental sign' in a way that the office of Reader is not.

It is, of course, open to all Readers to offer themselves, on advice and through their incumbents, for selection for ordination training. Although a Reader may be clear that he or she is not called to priestly ministry, the option of the permanent diaconate has not effectively been available in most dioceses. Greater encouragement, on the part of the clergy and diocesan vocations advisors, to consider this step, may well be appropriate – accompanied, as always, by prayerful discernment and confidential consultation at parochial, diocesan and national levels.

The obvious overlap of ministerial tasks between Readers and deacons (and more broadly between deacons and Ordained Local Ministers, with their particular form of training and restricted licenses) need not lead us to question the value of either Reader ministry or of the diaconate. The issue of overlap is not just one for the ministry of deacons, but has wider implications. Rather, it leads us to re-affirm the need for theological clarity and consistency about the various ministries of the Church, lay and ordained. In the present report we have given substantial attention to biblical, theological and ecumenical resources in order to assist this.

Although Readers sometimes feel that their role has been squeezed by the expanding roles of the clergy and of other laity, they remain a distinctive ministerial *cadre* within the Church of England. Readers have retained their distinct identity as nationally and canonically recognised, theologically trained, liturgically adept, lay people. Their competent contribution in conducting worship and ministering the word is unquestioned. In the next section we attempt to give a comparable 'job description' for the renewed diaconate. Once again the phrase 'distinctive but not exclusive' seems appropriate. There is ample work for both Readers and deacons, in their distinctive ways, in the tasks of mission that God has given to the Church.

Authorized Lay Parish/Pastoral Assistants (LPAs)

Authorized or recognized pastoral work by lay people has been a feature of the Christian Church for centuries, often organized in religious orders, charitable societies and missionary bodies. Even after the administration of the Poor Law had been removed from parish control, parishes in the nineteenth century supported teachers, nurses and visitors. Sisterhoods, monastic communities, nursing orders and orders of deaconesses flourished. Early in the twentieth century, national coordination and a scheme of training emerged for lay women's pastoral work. Today a considerable number of parishes support community, pastoral or youth workers.

In many parishes, LPAs (there is a variety of titles) are working with the clergy in liturgy, catechesis and pastoral care. Some parishes have introduced elders or recognized leaders of house groups. Other laity are involved in sector ministry, assisting chaplains in hospitals, prisons and educational institutions, for example. Diocesan or ecumenical social concern bodies employ lay pastoral workers of various kinds. Projects initiated by the churches for the benefit of the wider community, such as those supported by the Church Urban Fund, will sometimes employ lay people in a pastoral role.

LPAs have a defined ministry that is recognized locally and acknowledged by the bishop. Although there is no national policy for the calling, selection, training, commissioning and oversight of LPAs, in many dioceses there are guidelines and support structures for clergy and PCCs in setting up an LPA scheme. There are sensitive issues concerned with the selection, training, accountability and supervision of LPAs on which clergy need guidance and support.

LPAs may have part of their training in common with Readers and their functions may overlap with theirs, especially in assisting in church services. But generally the emphasis is less on study skills and verbal communication and more on practical, inter-personal skills. Some dioceses offer a Bishop's Certificate that qualifies but does not entitle a lay person to be appointed as an LPA. LPAs operate under the direction and oversight of the incumbent. Through visiting, they represent the parish church to the community and supplement the pastoral outreach of the clergy.

The work of LPAs impinges less on that of deacons than the ministry of Readers does. The emphasis is on carrying out a particular task in the local community, rather than on an ecclesiastical office. There is no suggestion that LPAs, for all their personal dedication and hard work, are called to a life-long ministry in that particular role. Their commission may well be time-limited and is related to local needs.

LPAs, like all Christians engaged in ministry, share in the authoritative commission – the *diakonia* – that belongs to the whole body and is appropriated according to the vocation and ministry of each. LPAs might well find their sense of confident commissioning strengthened if they had the opportunity to work alongside a renewed distinctive diaconate, linked to the bishop's oversight, in reaching out, in many forms of pastoral service, from the eucharistic heart of the Church's life to the needs of the community.

Local Ministry Teams (LMTs)

A further development in lay and ordained ministry is the burgeoning of Local Ministry Teams (LMTs). Sometimes these are connected with an Ordained Local Ministry (OLM) scheme. LMTs are obviously not the same as formal Team Ministries. They can operate within them or within a multi-parish benefice or in a sole cure parish. In practice LMTs usually operate benefice-wide. What is common to LMTs and Team Ministries today is the principle of collaborative ministry between clergy and laity. LMTs may include LPAs and active retired clergy, as well as stipendiary and non-stipendiary clergy and, of course, Readers.

There are degrees of formal commitment in LMTs. Some come into being progressively and in a low-key way, as gifts are discerned and affirmed; others are established with a fanfare of trumpets! Whether formal or informal, the litmus test of all LMTs is: mutual commitment to the team and its tasks; recognition by the parish through the PCC; shared responsibility in practice for the ministry of word, sacrament and pastoral care; regular meetings of the LMT (including the incumbent, of course) for sharing good practice, mutual support, supervision and prayer.

The calling of the team's members by the Holy Spirit through the Church is recognized in a commissioning service that has reference to the wider Church in the form of the diocese. Training of LMT members in particular skills before commissioning is followed by ongoing training, supervision and structures of accountability. LMTs need the leadership, encouragement and guidance of the incumbent or priest in charge who has the pastoral cure of souls and legal responsibilities entrusted to him/her.

In a parish with a climate that encourages vocations to various forms of Christian service, LMTs will evolve and will inevitably relate to the recognized ministry of, e.g. churchwardens and PCC members. In setting up LMTs, PCCs have to face the difficult but very necessary question of who is to be included and who is to be excluded. Do you involve in your LMT Sunday School teachers, youth group leaders and those who lead intercessions, but exclude churchwardens, vergers, choir leaders and most PCC officers?

If pastoral needs are to be shared at LMT meetings, the issue of confidentiality becomes crucial. Since not all engaged in Christian leadership in the parish can be members of the LMT, it makes sense for it to consist of those who are involved in the public, representative ministry of word, sacrament and pastoral care – while at the same time there is clear acknowledgement that there are many other, equally necessary lay ministries. Clergy need to beware of creating a parish hierarchy or two classes of parishioner. High profile deployment of LMTs (e.g. in liturgical processions) can cause resentment among those who are not included.

In addition, the balance between maintaining services and pastoral outreach to the unchurched needs to be kept under scrutiny. A healthy LMT needs a strategy for mission, agreed by the PCC, and should be involved in systematic pastoral contact with non-churchgoers.

An issue in the running of LMTs is where responsibility (oversight) lies. The incumbent receives the cure of souls, involving the ministry of word, sacrament and pastoral care, from the bishop, in such a way that pastoral responsibility is shared between bishop and incumbent ('both yours and mine'). Other ministers in LMTs assist in this ministry of word, sacrament and pastoral care. Yet one must always be clear that this ministry is not in some sense the property of the clergy, but belongs to the Church as the Body of Christ, being exercised through representative persons who are formally commissioned and empowered through ordination for this ministry. Since the PCC, together with the incumbent and the Churchwardens, is responsible for policy, finance and fabric, collaborative ministry must begin with the PCC.

LMTs are distinguished by collaborative ministry between ordained and lay ministers. In the welcome sense of common ownership and shared tasks (which is not the same as ultimate oversight – where the buck stops and who carries the can), LMTs need to be alert to the various vocations, gifts and recognized ministries that flourish within the Body of Christ as it is empowered by the Holy Spirit. Collaborative ministry is not about pretending that there is no difference between ordained and lay people. Least of all is it about assimilating certain lay people to the clergy by admitting them to the supposed privilege of close association with the clergy in the public eye – with the consequent distancing of everyone else.

Distinctive deacons will naturally take their place in LMTs where these are in operation. It is important that deacons do not thereby become assimilated to Lay Parish Assistants or to Readers and thereby take away from the ministry of such persons, as well as from their own diaconal ministry. The solution to the issue of overlap is surely not to curtail the flourishing of distinctive gifts and callings, exercised in a collaborative way, but to ground practice in a sound theology of representative ministry and in clarity about task and about lines of oversight to the bishop.

Conclusion: distinctive deacons and lay ministry

The possibility of encouraging a renewed or distinctive diaconate raises the important question of how a distinctive diaconate would enhance the mission and ministry of the whole body of the faithful (*laos*).

Conversely, the question should be asked, whether it would detract from or undermine the validity of lay ministries, especially those of Readers and LPAs. Clearly, nothing should be allowed to dampen the vitality of lay ministry in the Church today.

However, we are not aware of evidence in the extensive literature we have studied or in the various submissions we have received to suggest that effect. On the contrary, there is strong testimony that embodying sacramentally, so to speak, the *diakonia*, the commissioned service, of the Church in ordination, as an ecclesial sign of the *diakonia* of Jesus Christ, can enhance the sense of commissioned service among all the Church's ministers, lay and ordained.

In the General Synod debate that launched this work, the ecumenical representative from the Church of Scotland, the Revd Andrew McLellan (subsequently Moderator of the General Assembly), stated that a distinctive diaconate in his church 'energizes us all'. Bishop Sykes, in introducing the debate, said:

> In this matter, we ought, if possible, to think consistently: there simply are different vocations in Christ's Church ... It is right for our Church, as it was right for the medieval Church, to have a variety of designated ministries, with a publicly discernible face. It is right for our Church to continue and to esteem God's gift of 'diverse orders', of bishops, priests and deacons. There are drawbacks to the institution of order and ordination; there are temptations to self-importance in the office; but the issue of whether there is or is not a distinctive work for lifelong deacons, as for priests and bishops, ought not to become a moment for raising general anxieties about the devaluing of lay vocation. (*Report of Proceedings*, 1998, pp. 857f)

In the same debate Professor Hannaford said:

> The diaconate, like the other orders of the ministry, exists as a sacramental focus or channel for the life and mission of the whole community of faith. The confusion in the case of the diaconate is more acute because its name is derived from that general New Testament word for ministry. Progress can only be made if we get beyond this confusion and recognise that there is a *diakonia* which is proper to the order of deacons, just as there is a *diakonia* that is proper to the other orders of ministry. (*Ibid.*, pp. 862f)

The touchstone of a renewed diaconate is whether it builds up the diverse gifts and callings of the members of the Body of Christ.

As *Eucharistic Presidency* (1997) said of the ordained ministry as such, it is given to promote, release and clarify the ministry of the whole body (3.26). There is enough need of every kind in a world that cries out for redemption to engage fully the distinct gifts and callings of every form of ministry that the Spirit has given to the Church.

Distinctive deacons and particular ordained ministries

Our starting point must be the recognition that the ministry of bishops and presbyters is itself diaconal. That is inevitable, given that the Church itself is diaconal in nature. To say this is to say much more than that the Church and its ministers are called to serve. The Church and all its ministries are commissioned to be God's instrument, agent or ambassador. They are called to serve God and therefore the children of God. They are commissioned for a ministry of reconciliation, in order to gather into one body the people of God who are scattered abroad (2 Corinthians 5.18-19; John 11.52). Clearly, that is not an objection to an order that particularly embodies and expresses this diaconal character. Various facets of the Church's nature are particularly embodied in various ministries. Our concern here is not so much with the theological issue of how the threefold ordained ministry relates to what is true of the Church as such, as with the questions that arise when the functions of different ministries appear to be rather similar in practice.

A question to the Working Party

We turn at this point to address a specific submission to the Working Party by Oak Hill College Council. The Council wished to represent the views of that particular evangelical constituency in the Church of England that does not accept in conscience that women should be placed in positions of oversight *vis-à-vis* a community comprising both men and women, such as a parish (or congregation, as they might put it). This constituency grounds its position on a particular interpretation of biblical material about 'headship'. As the submission to the Working Party made clear, some evangelicals are looking for opportunities for a permanent, nationally recognized ministry for women that does not involve oversight. However, it is not entirely clear to us from the submission whether this would normally involve ordination.

Without embarking on a discussion of the theological merits of this view, it does seem to us that encouragement of a distinctive diaconate in the Church of England might meet this need provided certain collatoral questions were resolved. We certainly envisage that the renewed diaconate would take its essential character from the deacon's ministry as described in the Ordinal. In the nature of the case, deacons do not have ultimate responsibility for the cure of souls in a parish. As will become clear shortly, we do not expect distinctive deacons to be put in pastoral charge of parishes. In the strict sense, therefore, though they certainly will have a ministry of pastoral care and support, they will not have formal oversight.

However, our argument in this report may challenge certain assumptions behind the submission. It is, as we understand the biblical concept of *diakonia*, an essential aspect of the deacon's ministry (whether distinctive or transitional) to receive an authoritative commissioning for ministry. This commissioning is expressed in the ministry of the word in teaching, preaching and catechizing, and in the administration of baptism in certain circumstances, in officiating at marriages (normally after the first year) and in assisting at the celebration of the Eucharist in various ways (see below). Furthermore, in a renewed diaconate, the work of a deacon is closely associated with the ministry of the bishop and is appropriately linked with the bishop's leadership of the diocese. The evangelical constituency that is looking for a permanent 'non-headship' ministry for women would have to satisfy itself that it could accept these aspects of the diaconate (most of which are, of course, spelt out in the Ordinal). If so, a distinctive diaconate might meet this need.

Ordained Local Ministry

Most OLM schemes depend on a local team matrix (see above on LMTs) and it is the policy of the House of Bishops that OLMs should be part of a team. In OLM, the emphasis is on locally elicited vocation, selection criteria that are weighted differently than for stipendiary and conventional non-stipendiary ministry, locally based training and a bishop's licence that restricts the sphere of the OLM's ministry in terms of location and (sometimes) in terms of task (see *Stranger in the Wings*). There is overlap between the ministries of distinctive deacons and of OLMs and perhaps some blurring of roles in practice. Unlike deacons,

OLMs share eucharistic presidency with the incumbent and the bishop. But, like deacons, they do not share the cure (or care) of souls with the bishop: they are not given oversight or required to take ultimate responsibility for leadership in their communities. To that extent, there seems to be a tension with the central theme of the House of Bishops' document *Eucharistic Presidency* (1997) that pastoral oversight and eucharistic presidency properly belong together (though it might be said that, if OLMs are regarded as assistant curates, they may properly share in eucharistic presidency as a form of collegiality with the incumbent, just as conventional priested assistant curates do).

It is perhaps worth pointing out that dioceses that have set up an OLM scheme (with advice from the Ministry Division and the approval of the House of Bishops) may well not have considered the possibility of a distinctive diaconate. Just as there may be Readers who could suitably be called to ordination as distinctive deacons, there may be OLMs who could more suitably have been ordained to the distinctive diaconate. The pressure to provide eucharistic ministers can complicate the process of discernment of vocation.

Should the overlap of function between a distinctive diaconate and OLM inhibit dioceses that want to promote a renewed diaconate? We have already seen that overlap is endemic in Christian ministry, lay and ordained. But overlap is not the same as lack of clarity. The fact that the concept of OLM is still in its early days, coupled with some concern in the Church for greater rigour and consistency with regard to the theory and practice of OLM, suggests that a renewal of the diaconate, in line with biblical theology, ecumenical developments and contemporary needs, should not be deflected by the question of overlap with OLM.

chapter 7

The renewed diaconate: towards a ministerial profile

So far in our report we have taken stock of the diaconate as it now exists in the Church of England and we have looked at models and practices of *diakonia* in the Anglican Communion, the communion of Porvoo churches, and in the wider ecumenical scene. We have considered the renewal of the theology of ministry, both lay and ordained, in the Christian Church today and we have noted the remarkable convergence in ecumenical theology of the diaconate, stimulated by fresh research on the New Testament writings. We have sketched the mission context of ministry today and suggested that a renewed diaconate would have a special role in the Church's mission, which must always hold together the evangelistic, the pastoral and the liturgical. Finally, we have explored issues concerning the relation of a renewed diaconate to other recent developments in lay and ordained ministries in the Church of England. We have argued throughout that there is a distinctive but not exclusive ministry for a renewed diaconate 'for such a time as this'.

Now we must put flesh on the bones and translate the theology into practice. Can we draw up a model 'job description'? What would the ministerial profile of the diaconate as we envisage it actually look like? What do distinctive deacons do and what, in our view, should they not be expected to do? Both ways of looking at the question are important.

As we have already made clear (see pp. 2, 6, 7), we regard our proposals as standing in continuity with the classical Ordinal of the Church of England, which comprises one of the historic formularies of our church (Canon C 15: Preface to the Declaration of Assent). This is substantially the Ordinal of 1550, with a new Preface added in 1662. (This is, of course, the Ordinal that is bound together with *The Book of Common Prayer*.) Furthermore, as we have also emphasized, we believe that our proposals are fully consonant with the current Ordinal that forms part of the Alternative Service Book 1980. It is worth quoting that in full once again:

> A deacon is called to serve the Church of God, and to work with its members in caring for the poor, the needy, the sick, and all who are in trouble. He is to strengthen the faithful, search out the careless and indifferent, and to preach the word of God in the place to which he is licensed. A deacon assists the priest under whom he serves, in leading the worship of the people, especially in the administration of the Holy Communion. He may baptize when required to do so. It is his general duty to do such pastoral work as is entrusted to him.

Here there is a sense of the deacon being fully involved in, and not standing apart from the life and mission of the people of God. A threefold ministry of word, sacrament and pastoral care is envisaged for the deacon. It is clear that, although the deacon has a distinctive ministry, he (or she) does not have the cure of souls but assists those who do. However, the statement does not reflect the recently discovered insight that in Scripture *diakonia* is the service of God's Church because it is primarily the service of God. Moreover, while the relationship to the parish priest is emphasized, regrettably it is not expressed in a collegial way. It would have been better to have shown that the deacon has a distinctive ministry, alongside the parish priest, albeit under his or her oversight. The deacon's relationship to the bishop is not explicit here, though it is of course implied by the fact that it is the bishop (and the bishop alone in the case of deacons) who is ordaining.

The two movements of the Church's mission – sending and gathering – are suggested by the references to caring for those in need and searching out those who have drifted away, on the one hand, and leading worship and strengthening the faithful, on the other. But, regrettably, there is no mention of the deacon's involvement in social issues of justice, community-building, etc., and of bringing these to the heart of the Church's life through the liturgy.

So, although this statement could benefit from some fine tuning and the making explicit of what is implicit, there are actually sufficient theological resources in the current ordinal to support the thrust of the present report. In this report, we are advocating an approach that is already recognized and to some extent practised.

The evidence from Scripture, history, ecumenical theology and the experience of our partner churches leads us to see the diaconate as a fundamental expression of apostolic ministry. Deacons are sent and commissioned by God. They serve the risen Christ, who is Lord and Head of the Church. Because they serve the Lord, they serve his people, both their fellow Christians and all God's children in their several needs. They are agents of the ministry of Christ himself.

The special role of deacons is to make connections and build bridges between the distinctive life, the *koinonia*, of the Body of Christ and the needs of the world. They can help build up the visibility of the Church by forging relationships, as ordained representative ministers, with the local community and – on a diocesan and regional basis – with civil society. For example, deacons can help to link the Church's mission with initiatives in urban regeneration or tackling rural deprivation.

Their go-between character also brings deacons into close association with the bishop and with the bishop's colleagues, the presbyters of the diocese. It also brings them into intimate contact with committed lay people and sets them alongside recognized lay ministries. The calling of deacons is to focus, to encourage and to help coordinate the *diakonia* (the divine commission) of the whole Church within the mission of God in the world and to do this in three ways: through the liturgy, through pastoral outreach and through catechetical work. The huge challenges that face the Church's mission today lead us to ask whether we have taken the diaconate as seriously as we should have done and to question more than ever its current mainly transitional function. Deacons can help the Church to connect. They are a major missing link in the Church's ministry and mission.

Like many other clergy, deacons today are involved in a wide range of creative and innovative activities, bringing the values of the gospel to the worlds of the arts, education, therapy, community development, and many more. While we honour all these forms of Christian service, we do not cite them all as models of diaconal ministry. We try to focus on what is specific to deacons, what they are ordained for, not on what they might become involved with as Christian individuals alongside lay people and other clergy. We identify the distinctive ministry of deacons by reference to the three criteria of the ministry of the word, the sacrament and pastoral care, where all three are exercised in a representative way under episcopal and presbyteral oversight.

It is worth underlining here that deacons should certainly take part in the conciliar life of the Church at every level and may stand for election to various synods. They should play a full part in deanery chapters and local clergy fraternals. Their ministry may particularly lend itself to ecumenical collaboration. In all these spheres, it is important that the distinctive voice of the diaconate should be heard.

The ministerial profile of the deacon will, then, include pastoral, liturgical and catechetical elements. These are not discrete elements in the life of the Church but are interrelated. They form the cycle of mission, a cycle that individuals may enter at any of the three points. All three are incorporated here in a missiological sense.

Pastoral

Pastoral care includes not simply the loving support of faithful members of the local Christian community, but also pastoral outreach to those (as the ASB Ordinal suggests) who have backslidden from church attendance or whose faith has become weak and troubled. By some accounts, more than half the population of England has drifted from earlier contact with the Christian Church. Such outreach must also, of course, include those who have had little past contact with the Church and for whom a link needs to be forged for the first time. The total constituency of the unchurched comprises a vast mission field where deacons, working with lay people who can devote themselves to this work, are needed. In the present state of our society, where there is a hunger for spiritual meaning combined with an indifference towards the institutional face of the churches, pastoral outreach is at the cutting edge of mission and should be seen as a form of evangelism. Church Army Evangelists model a compassionate form of pastoral outreach in the cause of mission. Deacons also may be encouraged to specialize in evangelism. This role is certainly consistent with the understanding of the deacon as an out-reaching minister of the gospel. But a rounded view of evangelism will not detach it from the pastoral mission of the Church or from the ministry of the word and sacraments, to both of which deacons are ordained. The bridging, go-between aspect of the deacon's ministry becomes particularly significant at this point.

The Church builds trust and respect in the community for its message when it gets alongside individuals, households and local organizations and institutions in a personal way. General pastoral visitation of the parish is perhaps now one of the weakest aspects of the Church's ministry, for various reasons. But the fact is that people respond best of all to a personal approach. Words alone cut little ice. Loving concern and practical support are the best ambassadors of the gospel in a largely post-Christian culture.

In this context, the vital pastoral role that deacons can play will vary according to their individual gifts and the needs of the parish. In teams of ordained and lay ministers, deacons may specialize in one or more particular areas of pastoral ministry, such as:

- Having a special care for the poor, the sick, the lonely and those who are ground down by adverse circumstances or by the pressures of life at home or work.

- Breaking new ground, as go-between persons, reaching parts of the community that are largely untouched by the regular ministry of the Church ('a safe foothold to a place beyond'); representing the Church and its Lord at the margins of society and beyond the normal boundaries of the Church, 'reaching into the forgotten corners of the world' (for example, making contact with hostels for the homeless and with families in bed and breakfast accommodation).

- Being an authorized prophetic voice on behalf of justice and working for change in oppressive and unjust structures.

- Helping to set up new networks and to gather fresh resources for pastoral outreach, so helping to draw individuals and families into the community of the Church.

- Modelling and encouraging outreach to help motivate some less confident lay people to witness to their faith by entering into collaboration with them.

- Leading and coordinating general pastoral visiting in the parish, keeping track of new arrivals in the neighbourhood and of special pastoral needs and providing continuity and coherence.

- Having a special concern for young families, especially among the unchurched; working to bring them within the ambit of the Church's means of grace through pram services, crib services, parent and toddler groups, etc.

- Developing a special ministry in schools and youth organizations, hospitals and prisons.

- Being the focal ministry person, in collaboration with the parish priest, in a particular area within the benefice where the deacon, but not the priest happens to live.

Liturgical

Deacons embody the *sine qua non* of the Church's mission: that it should be grounded in and never lose touch with the liturgical life of the Church, made up of word and sacrament, praise and intercession. Deacons have a distinctive ministry in the celebration of the liturgy, assisting the bishop or priest who is presiding. In particular, in their go-between role, they bring into worship the concerns and hopes of all God's children that these may be lifted up to the throne of grace.

The deacon's liturgical ministry is recognized in the rubrics of *Common Worship* and may include:

- Ministering at the celebration of the Eucharist in ways that are appropriate to the life of the community and without excluding the ministry of lay people: reading the Gospel, leading the prayers of penitence, the intercessions and the acclamations of the people, inviting the exchange of the peace, serving at the altar, administering Holy Communion, and sending out the people with the liturgical dismissal.

- Conducting the daily offices and other non-eucharistic liturgical services, especially Morning and Evening Prayer.

- Officiating at baptism at the request of the parish priest.

- Ordering the church or cathedral liturgically for the community's worship, with special regard to preparing the font and the altar, supporting and guiding the sacristan or virger.

- Conducting house and hospital communions with the sacrament reserved for the sick and housebound and officiating at services of the word with the administration of Holy Communion ('extended communion').

- Assisting and (except in their first year) officiating at marriages.

- Conducting funeral services and burials.

- Ministering to the sick and the dying with prayers.

Catechetical

Deacons in the Church of England are ordained also to the ministry of the word of God. They are called and trained to preach and to teach. They carry out this ministry in collaboration with and under the oversight of the parish priest and both deacon and priest are subject to the oversight of the bishop who is called to be a guardian of sound doctrine. This aspect of the deacon's ministry overlaps with those of Reader, presbyter and bishop. Once again, there is scope for specialization according to need and gift, including:

- Coordinating and monitoring faith-development courses, such as Alpha and Emmaus, and Lent courses (including working with other churches where these courses are run ecumenically) and working with the parish priest to follow up the opportunities these provide.

- Preparing candidates (or their parents) for baptism.

- Preaching in the liturgy.

- Conducting Confirmation preparation.

- Preparing couples for marriage.

- Where some of these catechetical tasks are carried out by trained lay people, to help train the trainers, to support and guide them in this work.

- Supporting and guiding lay people's involvement in such children's activities as After School and Holiday Clubs.

- Specialist counselling, seen as being on behalf of the Church, to those diagnosed with HIV/AIDS or those addicted to various forms of substance abuse.

- Training volunteers to befriend families in need.

- Representing the Church's concerns and priorities, on behalf of the bishop, in areas of community action and in relation to major institutions within the diocese (local and regional government, urban regeneration initiatives, the health service, the world of education, the voluntary sector, etc.). Such specific areas of mission should be decided in discussion with the bishop before ordination and licensing.

- Training and teaching roles within the diocese, archdeaconry or deanery. (It would seem appropriate for a person carrying out this form of the ministry of the word, with the bishop's commission, and who was not called to oversight and to presidency at the Eucharist, to remain a deacon.)

Clarifying the role of deacon

In relation to ordained ministry, it is important that the advent of a renewed diaconate should help to clarify the differentiation of the threefold ministry and other authorized ministries. It is widely recognized that a one-year transitional diaconate does not enhance clarity about this ministry. Questions are frequently raised as to whether the reality of the deacon's ministry can be authentically experienced in this brief period. Although overlap is endemic in all forms of ministry, a renewed diaconate should not add to existing grey areas and blurred edges but should assist clarity.

In relation to lay ministry, a renewed diaconate should on no account absorb expressions of ministry that are entrusted to lay people. In parishes where lay ministry already flourishes, deacons will help to support, guide and coordinate this. It is not for them to seek to control it or to try to take it over. They will be well advised to be supportive in the background until their enabling and training gifts are invited. In parishes where lay ministry has barely got off the ground, deacons will focus, model and pioneer expressions of ministry to which lay people may be called, helping to release talents and energy within the community and then taking a back seat as much as possible.

Although deacons must be rooted in the liturgical life of the Church, especially the Eucharist, the main focus of the work that they do will be in the wider world where they represent the Church as an ordered community under the leadership of bishops and priests. Their liturgical role can helpfully be seen as an oblation of this ministry to God. They should not become simply liturgical functionaries. Mission remains the litmus test of ministry and a deacon is primarily a missionary.

Deacons in administration?

It is sometimes suggested that deacons might specialize in church administration, perhaps in support of the bishop. The roles of bishop's chaplain and of archdeacon are sometimes cited. Of course, it is not the administrative duties alone of either a bishop's chaplain or an archdeacon that make it appropriate for that person to be ordained. One does not need to be ordained to do office work or other administrative chores or to liaise with the bishop's co-workers or to organize meetings or to draft letters for the bishop.

It is primarily the liturgical role of the bishop's chaplain – combined perhaps with a pastoral role to individuals on behalf of the bishop – that makes ordination appropriate. If the chaplain is not to have pastoral charge of a parish and is not required to preside at the Eucharist, then it makes sense for him or her to be a deacon.

It might well be appropriate for a person who leads and coordinates a charitable agency of the Church to be a deacon, provided it can be seen in each case that it is a role that belongs properly to the ordained. A commissioning to direct work that is primarily pastoral in nature, provided that it included some elements of the ministry of the word and/or the sacraments, would seem to fit this criterion.

Archdeacons in deacons' orders have been a tradition in Orthodoxy and have been reinvented recently in the Episcopal Church of the USA and in the Diocese of Brisbane. However, this practice seems questionable to us. Even if an archdeacon is never going to preside at the Eucharist, which would seem an undue restriction of that ministry, he or she certainly exercises oversight, sometimes in the form of discipline, on behalf of the diocesan bishop. Presbyters directly share the bishop's oversight; deacons do not. The Church of England's Canons (C 22) emphasize the jurisdiction of the archdeacon as ordinary and that would seem to be the basis of the canonical requirement that archdeacons shall be in priest's orders.

Deacons in pastoral charge?

For similar reasons, we would not expect a deacon to be placed in pastoral charge of a parish, even temporarily. Deacons are not ordained to oversight but to a ministry of assistance to and collaboration with those in oversight. This restriction, that is inherent in the nature of their order, should not be taken as preventing deacons from showing leadership in specific areas of Church work or from being put forward by the incumbent as the focal pastoral person in a particular community within, say, a multi-parish benefice. A degree of prominence is entailed in any representative ministry, whether lay or ordained, but this is a different matter from having formal pastoral charge, the cure of souls and being accountable to the bishop for that. When deacons are put in positions of oversight, serious distortion of their calling ensues. We are clear that pastoral charge is one area that is definitely not right for the deacon.

Deacons as ministers in secular employment

We are not assuming in this report that distinctive deacons will necessarily be non-stipendiary. But obviously some, perhaps a considerable proportion, will be self-financing. So there will be deacons who will exercise their diaconal ministry in church and in the parish community but will have a so-called secular job as well. Some may have the opportunity to exercise a diaconal ministry (one that is liturgical, pastoral and catechetical) in their place of work with the permission of their employer and the goodwill of their colleagues. But this is a sensitive area and demands wisdom, restraint and patience until the Lord opens the door that no one can shut (cf. Revelation 3.8).

Looking at the matter another way, what about ordaining deacon a person who has a noted ministry, as a lay person, in their place of work? Once again, we must not appear to detract from the integrity of lay ministry and witness. We would not expect a Minister in Secular Employment to be ordained either deacon or priest unless there was a specific representative ministry of word, sacrament and pastoral care that could be discerned in that person's work situation. All Christians serve the Lord in their daily calling, whether at home, in the local community, or in another place of work. They witness to their faith in various informal ways. We would be looking for a special representative role, normally recognized in some way by the person's employer and work colleagues, before we would consider ordination appropriate.

Having said that, if a representative ministry of leading worship, teaching the faith and extending pastoral care should develop, it would seem right for the individual concerned to have his or her vocation to the diaconate tested. Given that recognized role in certain cases, we would judge ordination to the diaconate, rather than to the priesthood, to be appropriate for a person who would not be sharing directly in pastoral oversight and would not be presiding at the Eucharist.

chapter 8

Implications for selection, training and deployment

In conclusion, we offer some guidelines, formulated in the light of discussion with senior staff of the Ministry Division, on the implications of our recommendations for the selection, training and deployment of a renewed diaconate.

Selection

At present there is a standard set of eight criteria, laid down by the House of Bishops, for selection for all forms of ordained ministry and for Accredited Lay Workers. These criteria are interpreted with a degree of flexibility in the selection of permanent Non-stipendiary and Ordained Local Ministers, with regard to leadership potential and collaborative and academic aptitudes respectively. We suggest that the same set of criteria should be applied in a nuanced way to the selection of distinctive deacons in the light of our description above of the deacon's ministry.

The selectors would be expected to press the candidates to give reasons why they were offering for the distinctive diaconate rather than for the transitional diaconate and then the presbyterate. By the same token, selectors would need to press candidates for the transitional diaconate and then the presbyterate to give reasons why they were not offering for the distinctive diaconate.

During the selection process there is scope for discerning a possible change of sponsorship category.

It is, of course, the bishop's decision, on advice, whether to ordain a deacon to the presbyterate. In practice, the existence nationally of a distinctive diaconate would offer the bishop greater flexibility with regard to the timing of this step. We believe that taking the diaconate seriously implies that ordinands should not assume that they will automatically be ordained to the presbyterate after a year.

In the event of a distinctive deacon's vocation developing to the point where the individual wished, with guidance, to offer him- or herself for ordination to the presbyterate, a further process of selection, either within the diocese or via the Candidates' Committee of the Ministry Division, would be called for.

Training

Does a distinctive diaconate need a distinctive training? We believe that both those candidating ultimately for the presbyterate and those candidating for the distinctive diaconate should undergo a basic common training, which will include preparation for the diaconate, since all are to be ordained deacon. In addition, there should be special alternative modules, designed in the light of this report, for those selected for the distinctive diaconate. It would seem appropriate for the Theological Education and Training Committee of the Ministry Division to consider this aspect and to offer advice to the House of Bishops.

One issue that will arise, especially in the early days of a distinctive diaconate, is that of cohort size, the minimum viable number of candidates for effective training together. For this reason, the House of Bishops may wish, in the first instance, to limit its recognition of institutions for diaconal training purposes.

However, the Working Party believes that all training for ordination should take the diaconate seriously and that this should be reflected in accreditation procedures, particularly in submissions under the ACCM 22 arrangements.

The Working Party also wishes to discourage any assumption that distinctive deacons will normally be trained on regional courses rather than in residential colleges.

Deployment

Both stipendiary and non-stipendiary ministry should be open to distinctive deacons. It should not be assumed that they will be unpaid, any more than that they will be female. Given our understanding of what it would be appropriate for distinctive deacons to do and not to do, we envisage that they will tend to be deployed in ministry teams (especially where there is an emphasis on outreach to those at the margins of the community) or on the staff of major parish churches or cathedrals. The distinctiveness of their ministry will complement the roles of priests, Readers and LPAs.

Stipendiary deacons are already part of the Clergy Allocation scheme under the Sheffield formula and will continue to be so. Non-stipendiary deacons are not included in the scheme.

Like others sponsored for training for stipendiary ministry, those selected for training for stipendiary diaconal ministry will require an assurance of a post in the sponsoring diocese, unless they ask to be released from the diocesan link.

We recommend that distinctive deacons should be placed on the same scale of stipend as other assistant clergy, with flexibility to recognize special areas of responsibility.

Continuing Ministerial Education of distinctive deacons, especially in years 1–4 after ordination, should reflect their special ministry as sketched in this report.

In the first few years of a distinctive diaconate, at least, the Ministry Division could helpfully set up national conferences in support of sponsoring bishops, Diocesan Directors of Ordinands and training incumbents.

Bibliography

Advisory Council for the Church's Ministry	*Deacons Now*, report of a Church of England Working Party concerned with women in ordained ministry, 1990.
Anglican–Reformed International Commission	*God's Reign and Our Unity*, the report of the, SPCK/ The Saint Andrew Press, 1984.
ARCIC [Anglican–Roman Catholic International Commission]	*The Final Report*, CTS/SPCK, 1982.
Board for Social Responsibility of the Church of England	'Guidelines for Faith Communities when Dealing with Disasters', Church House/Home Office, 1997.
Board of Education of the Church of England	*Formal Lay Ministry*, 1999.
G. Borgegård and C. Hall (eds)	*The Ministry of the Deacon, 1. Anglican–Lutheran Perspectives*, Nordic Ecumenical Council, 1999.
G. Borgegård, O. Fanuelsen and C. Hall (eds)	*The Ministry of the Deacon, 2. Ecclesiological Explorations*, Nordic Ecumenical Council, 2000.
S.-E. Brodd	'Diaconia through church history: five ecclesiological models', in S.-E. Brodd *et al.*, *The Theology of Diaconia*, Diakonistiftelsen Samariterhemmet, 1999.
J. N. Collins	*Diakonia: Re-interpreting the Ancient Sources*, Oxford University Press, 1990.

64

General Synod of the Church of England — *Report of Proceedings* vol. 29 no. 3 (November 1998), Church House Publishing.

House of Bishops of the Church of England — *Bishops in Communion*, Church House Publishing, 2000.

House of Bishops of the Church of England — *Deacons in the Ministry of the Church*, Church House Publishing, 1988.

House of Bishops of the Church of England — *Eucharistic Presidency: A Theological Statement by the House of Bishops of the General Synod* (GS 1248), Church House Publishing, 1997.

C. Hall (ed.) — *The Deacon's Ministry*, Gracewing, 1991.

P. C. Rodger and L. Fischer (eds) — *Fourth World Conference on Faith and Order: The Report from Montreal 1963*, WCC/SCM, 1964.

E. Schweizer — *Church Order in the New Testament*, SCM Press, 1961.

T. K. Seim — *The Double Message,* T. & T. Clark, 1994.

J.R. Wright — 'Sequential or cumulative orders vs. direct ordination', *Anglican Theological Review*, LXXV: 2, 1993, pp. 246–51.

Baptism, Eucharist and Ministry, WCC, 1982 [BEM]

Basic Norms for the Formation of Permanent Deacons and *Directory for the Ministry and Life of Permanent Deacons*, Liberia Editrice Vaticana, Vatican City, 1998.

Called to Witness and Service: The Reuilly Common Statement with Essays on Church, Eucharist and Ministry, Church House Publishing, 1999 [Reuilly].

Commitment to Mission and Unity: Report of the Informal Conversations Between the Methodist Church and the Church of England, Church House Publishing and Methodist Publishing House, 1996.

Deacons of the Gospel: A Vision for Today, a Ministry for Tomorrow, a report of the Working Group on Ministry, a Deliverance to the 2001 General Assembly of the Church of Scotland.

The Diaconate as Ecumenical Opportunity, Hanover Report of the Anglican–Lutheran International Commission, Anglican Communion Publications,1996.

The Meissen Agreement: Texts, Council for Christian Unity, 1992 [Meissen].

Ministers of the Gospel: A Policy Statement for the Board of Ministry, a Deliverance to the 2000 General Assembly of the Church of Scotland, Church of Scotland Board of Practice and Procedure, 2000.

The Niagara Report: Report of the Anglican–Lutheran Consultation on Episcope 1987 (ACC/LWF), Church House Publishing, 1988 [Niagara].

Sharing in the Apostolic Communion: The Report of the Anglican–Methodist International Commission, World Methodist Council, USA, 1996.

Stranger in the Wings: A Report on Local Non-Stipendiary Ministry, Church House Publishing, 1998.

Together in Mission and Ministry: The Porvoo Common Statement with Essays on Church and Ministry in Northern Europe, Church House Publishing, 1993 [Porvoo].

Index

~

CPSIA information can be obtained
at www.ICGtesting.com
Printed in the USA
BVHW052010310120
571148BV00017B/161